Outlines

k.d. lang

Other works by Rose Collis

Portraits To The Wall
(Cassell 1994)

A Trouser-Wearing Character: The Life and Times of Nancy Spain
(Cassell 1997)

Outlines

k.d. lang

ROSE COLLIS

Absolute Press

First published in 1999 by Absolute Press
Scarborough House, 29 James Street West,
Bath, Somerset, England BA1 2BT
Tel: 01225 316013 Fax: 01225 445836
Email: outlines@absolutepress.demon.co.uk

Distributed in the United States of America and Canada by
Stewart, Tabori and Chang
115 West 18th Street, New York, NY 10011

Series editor Nick Drake

Cover and text design by Ian Middleton

Cover printed by Devenish and Co. Bath
Printed by The Cromwell Press, Trowbridge

ISBN 1 899791 47 7

Contents

Introduction	7
A curious soul astray	13
A truly western experience	25
Craving it, getting it	37
This year's model	53
Lifted by love	65
Old addictions	81
High time for a detour	91
Notes	107
Discography	111
Websites	111
Picture credits	112

Acknowledgments

My thanks to everyone who has been of help and support during the writing of this book, especially my editor Nick Drake, Jon Croft, Sally McMahon, Tom Sargant, Peter Burton, Paul Boyd, Mark Peters, Heather Playle, Gillian Rodgerson, Emma at Cowlick and Bel's Cyber Café.

My special love and thanks to Radcliffe, for bravely defying the odds and hanging on – much loved and missed by everyone who knew her. Especially me. This book is dedicated to her, and, with all respect, to the late Dusty Springfield.

Introduction

'I'm too young to have a biography done … there's nothing interesting about me …'
k.d. lang

Fine. This isn't a biography.

But it's been written because, contrary to what the subject says herself, there is plenty that always has been, and always will be, interesting about k.d. lang – even if she never makes another recording, never plays another show, and retires to live in domestic bliss with her girlfriend, raising puppies and pumpkins.

Not interesting?
Come off it, girl.

People who don't think they're very interesting don't announce at the age of 13 that they're going to become a major singing star. They don't, like a country and western Quixote, tilt at the windmills of Nashville as they challenge the conventional wisdom that dictates what women singers in that genre should represent. They don't put their careers on the line by coming out as gay, by being an active AIDS campaigner and animal rights supporter, before such causes became 'fashionable'. They don't appear on the cover of *Vanity Fair* being pandered to by the world's most famous supermodel. And, just as they hit a rich vein of success, don't switch musical and personal styles as and when they damn well feel like it.

Fate must have a reason. How else do you explain the phenomenon that was the 1992 metamorphosis of k.d. lang from a kooky, angel-voiced country singer with an aversion to bouffant hair and high heels, to the most famous lesbian in the world – a headline-grabbing, award-scooping singer and an idol desired by maids and Madonnas alike? From a big-boned, tomboyish gal to a *Vanity Fair* cover girl: the one dyke who many straight women, when playing truth or dare, admit they wouldn't throw out of bed. From being the product of a tiny, beef-producing town in rural Canada, where the cows sure outnumber the cowhands, to committed vegetarian and animal rights supporter. From smalltown values to self-professed 'pantheism'.

No, nothing very interesting in all that ...

k.d. lang is a bundle of contradictions, a lower-cased square peg who doesn't appear to want to fit into any hole, round or otherwise. She's reeled and polka-ed her way from performance art, to anarchic Country and Western, dotsey-doed with Nashville, worn her heartbreak on her sleeve to become a Grammy award-winning chanteuse – only pausing for breath occasionally to add to the bits'n'pieces acting career that's never been quite as on-song as everything else she's done.

She's always said she prefers the company of animals, that 'humans are one of my least favourite species on the planet'[1] – which is completely understandable. Then again, she's been adamant that she is 'not attracted' to reading, pays no attention to the news, never looks at papers, magazines or books, just a dictionary – which is in no way understandable. Most curious is her claim that she didn't fall in love, didn't lose control of her emotions, until she was 30 – all over an unobtainable woman who was the muse for her greatest critical and commercial success.

First real love at 30? This was hardly following the tradition of lovelorn country and torch singers whose footsteps she followed in, who had forged entire careers out of their private heartaches. No pain, no gain.

Her reputation as one of the finest white female vocalists of the late 20th century, up there with her idols Peggy Lee and Patsy Cline, cannot be denied. And, like another of her heroines, fellow Canadian Joni Mitchell, k.d. lang's voice has been the passport on her musical odyssey.

Many vocalists have had aspirations to hop from genre to genre, but few have had the voice or the guts to pull it off. However, history may yet show that the very things she's overt about, and proud of, that have marked out her personal quirkiness — her sexuality, her vegetarianism, her identity as a Canadian — still kept the mainstream at arm's length. Unlike some of the stars who jumped on the nineties lesbian chic bandwagon, there's no teasy-weasy ambiguity about her sexuality: it's full-frontal, sit-on-yer-face lesbianism. But then her all-organic, animal-preserving, extra-crunchy-granola lifestyle, almost as pure as her voice, is at odds with the lifestyle of many urban dykes to whom she might otherwise appeal. As one Canadian lesbian journalist has remarked: 'There's nothing so boring as a self-righteous Canadian ...' In June 1994, *Vox* ran an unprecedented nine-page special on 'the new lesbian cool', including the musical flipside of lang: West Coast US dyke punk bands, Tribe 8, Random Violet, Malibu Barbie and Aunt Fister. But the main picture accompanying the piece was of Ellyot Dragon from queercore band Sister George tearing a picture of k.d. lang in half. So, er, could that possibly mean that Ellyot wasn't a l-l-l-l ... langster, then?

> *'We hate k.d. lang! Just because she's a dyke people say, you must support her. But she's awful, terrible. Her music is appaling! She should be shot.'*[2]

We'll take that as a 'no', then ...

For a very long time, there were many lesbians who neither knew nor cared about some kitsch country and western singer who was in their midst.

★ ★ ★ ★ ★ ★

If you work behind a bar, you get to see and hear a lot of strange things. People tell you their stories, sometimes you tell them yours. But mostly, you smile and you serve and you watch and you listen.

And there's one they still tell in a little place just outside the centre of Brighton. They swear it's true, it really is, that's the way it happened, it really did ...

Back around 1991, 1992, there used to be a women's night on Sunday evenings in the basement bar of The Sanctuary, *a café in Hove.* Simone On Top, *they called it. You don't need to know why, you can use your imagination.*

If you were a stranger in town for the weekend, and wanting to check out where the girls were, chances are you'd end up at Simone's. *Someone was sure to point you in the right direction. Everyone ended up at* Simone's, *sooner or later.*

One Sunday evening, a tall, handsome woman came down the stairs and into the basement bar, alone. The place was quite busy, as it usually was — there was nowhere else for women to hang out together for a drink on a Sunday night. And that's what someone had told the tall dark stranger. She'd ended up at Simone's *for a beer and that's what she headed to the bar to get. And that's where she stayed. All evening. All alone. No one came up and tried to make polite conversation with her; they didn't know who the hell she was, they'd never seen her face in there before. She never went there again. But they would see her face again … and again … and again … on posters, on TV, in magazines, in newspapers. Her image was everywhere.*

And it was only her image which would return to The Sanctuary.

But, as far as anyone knows, k.d. lang hasn't dropped in for a beer again.

★ ★ ★ ★ ★ ★

It hardly seems possible now that k.d. lang could go walking into any ginjoint anywhere in the Western world and not cause so much as a stir. But it really was not so very long ago, that she could come and go very quietly, no fuss, no muss. An *Independent* journalist recalled seeing her at Paris airport in 1993, about to fly to Los Angeles. There was no entourage, no personal assistant, no hand luggage — just a first-class ticket 'crumpled up in her jacket pocket'.[3] *Plus ça change.*

But you see, once upon a time, k.d. lang was a big secret.
Being a fan of hers was a big secret.
Liking country and western music was a big secret.
And coming out as either wasn't easy in those days.

'Hey, have you heard that k.d. lang single ... k.d. lang, she's this new country singer ... oh, I just heard it on the radio a couple of times ... have you seen what she looks like? ... what do you mean, how do I know ... yeah, OK, I have bought the album actually, but it's not exactly country and western ... no, she doesn't sing bloody D.I.V.O.R.C.E songs ... she's done a really great version of 'Rose Garden' ... anyway, she looks really dykey, that's the point ... she has to be, I know it! I don't know what it is about her, but you can tell she's just − kind of different ...'

Sure, some people might have guessed − there are always a few tell-tale signs that someone is a l-l-l ... Loretta Lynn fan. And even once you got past admitting what you were, it was tougher to reveal that you'd lost your heart to a big-boned gal with a moniker that suggested she was related to a certain famous family psychiatrist. And she wasn't even a Nashville big-boned gal, either − she came from *Canada*, of all places.

And, as any fule no, bears, snow and maple leaves have naff-all to do with country and western ... don't they?

K.D. WITH LULU THE COW, SUPPORTING PETA AND CAUSING CONTROVERSY

A curious soul astray

With the release of *A Truly Western Experience* in 1984, k.d. lang set out on her Grand Tour, a musical and personal journey that took her to the places and people she dreamed of reaching since she was 13. And, as is often the way with great singers, this journey began in a place which bore no outwardly apparent signs of having a claim to fame.

If you're going to be a major singing star, it's definitely a very good thing to hail from a slightly dysfunctional or unorthodox background, you know the sort of thing: Elvis Presley, the surviving twin son of po' white trash, raised in a one-room shack in Tupelo. Celine Dion, the youngest of 14 children, married to a man old enough to be her father ... Of course, if you're going to be a country singer, this sort of stuff is virtually *de rigeur* if Nashville is to clasp you to its rhinestoned bosom. Look at Loretta Lynn: born in a Kentucky hollow, married at 13, a mother of four at 18. And then there's Tammy Wynette – she ... oh heck, there isn't room for all *her* stuff here.

So it figured that the woman who became k.d. lang started out as Kathryn Dawn Lang from a tiny Canadian town, with a population of less than 700 people (plus thousands of cattle), where, as she later recalled, 'I went to school with the same twenty people for twelve years'.[4]

Her parents, Fred and Audrey, married after World War II, and moved to Consort, which had one TV station, one radio station and no cinema. Fred opened a drugstore, the IDA Drug Mart, and Mom became a teacher at the local school. k.d. lang has often alluded to the misconception of life in a smalltown as boring and unconventional, and refuted this with her observations that, out of 700 people, it's just as likely that 99% of them would be as eccentric as any big-city folk.

In which case, the Lang family served as the perfect microcosm of Consort: three out of the four Lang children turned out glad to be gay. Three out of four – that's not bad going for one smalltown family.

This includes her sister Keltie Rae, three years her senior, who runs the farm they share outside Vancouver, along with horses, goats, a pig and, at one time, kd's adored mutt, Stinker – who, like her mistress, also underwent a radical name-change. She started life known as Gillian.

When they were older, and knew they were sisters in more than one sense of the word, lang says she and Keltie used to play spot-the-dyke together: 'When we saw a woman in a leather jacket or a suit, we'd freak out. We'd look for little symbols on TV shows ...'[5]

Looking for 'little symbols' in the young Kathy Dawn wasn't exactly hard. She was the little girl who was always showing-off and who told her boy playmates that she, too, was going home to her wife. She did lots of tomboy stuff with her dad, shooting and Skidooing. She was, in her own words, the 'class clown. And the big athlete ... just a bored person trying to involve herself in everything that was going on'.[6] This included becoming a local star in volleyball and javelin.

She was only 12 when Fred upped and left the family, and then three of her classmates were killed in an accident. lang clammed up about her childhood for nearly 20 years, until she went into therapy, after the release of *Ingenue* seemed to release her. She said the analysis had helped her identify her 'constant craving' as 'a product of abandonment'.[7]

Brother John also left the confines of Consort, following the hippy trail to India. When he returned to Alberta, he brought back with him the novel (for a cattle-farming town) concept of a vegetarian diet, introducing his kid sister to the delights of kormas and dhal. While she was learning about vegetarian diets, she was also being nurtured with kitsch and camp. Her childhood idol was Julie Andrews in the sixties, the Langs drove for four hours across gravel roads to Edmonton to see *The Sound Of Music*. 'My favourite bit is when she's on the top of the hill at the beginning',[8] lang later revealed. So it was only fitting, then, that it was a nun, Sister Xavier, who gave piano lessons to the Lang offspring, encouraged the tomboy Kathy in her singing, and entered her for her first talent contest. Other Broadway musicals, from *Fiddler On The Roof* to *My Fair Lady*, made a significant impact on the young lang's consciousness, and her eclectic taste in music also took in sixties harmony duo The Caravelles, Trini Lopez and Peggy Lee.

In the fifties, Lee was the vocal heroine of Dusty Springfield; 20 years later, she was influencing another gay icon, budding chanteuse Kathy Dawn Lang. In years to come, she would always point to the classy, precise, uncluttered vocalizing of Lee as the touchstone of her own singing aspirations. 'One of the things I'm afraid of is over-singing, over-acting, over-emoting',[9] she would explain. She also considered Lee 'the Madonna of her day',[10] and it was Lee who lang chose to be photographed with for a *Rolling Stone* feature in the early nineties, on singers' heroes and heroines.

Another of lang's early heroines was Canada's own *Snowbird*, Anne Murray. Precociously, young Kathy Dawn sent her idol some lyrics, adding that she had permission to use them. Murray passed up the chance to do the first-ever cover of a k.d. lang song. She never replied to the letter. Amusingly, lang would later get revenge for this early 'snub'. She won the Canadian Juno Award for Best Country Female Vocalist of 1987 of which Anne Murray had been the recipient for the previous eight years in a row. Then, in November 1990, the Canadian Academy of Recording Arts and Sciences awarded lang their Female Artist of the Decade gong. Previous winner? Why, Anne Murray, of course ...

At 13, Kathy Dawn wrote her first song proper, 'Hoping All My Dreams Come True', and told anyone who would listen that she wanted to be a star. She would later explain that all this meant was, 'I want to sing, I want to be an artist'[11] but, then again, she was not averse to telling friends to keep hold of bits of paper she had signed, because those autographs would be worth something when she was famous.

K.D. (SEATED, SECOND FROM RIGHT) AND THE CONSORT HIGH SCHOOL
VOLLEYBALL TEAM

When she left Consort to study music at Red Deer Academy, it wasn't just
the music course she was interested in – it was the reputation of the
volleyball team, although she never actually made it on to the team, in more
ways than one.

At Red Deer, she became soulmates with another curious soul, Gary Elgar,
known as Drifter. She dabbled in performance art, doing her now-legendary
12-hour re-enactment of a heart transplant, and other performances which
seemed to involve rolling around the stage in a black plastic bag. Then Drifter
dropped out of college, and so did she, and took to hanging out with the
boys, all swagger and poise, taking off cross-country in her old car, doing
part-time Joe jobs. Then one day, Drifter decided to live up to his name, so
Kathy Lang moved to Edmonton and discovered the city's small gay scene –
and decided to get to work on making all her dreams come true. But to do

that, she needed some special men in her life – and she didn't take too many years to find them.

Larry Wanagas was the owner of Homestead recording studios in Edmonton when lang turned up for a band audition in late 1982. The gig turned out to be short-lived, unlike her partnership with Wanagas, who became her manager in early 1983. Then she had to get her very own band, which started life as The k.d. lang Band, and evolved into The Reclines – after she had some minor corrective surgery done on her name.

Of course, the lowercasing of k.d. lang had naff-all to do with a fondness for e e cummings – it's simply because she writes everything in lower case – and, possibly, because Kathy Dawn, as *The Guardian* put it so well, 'calls to mind page three girls and holiday reps'.[12] So k.d. lang it would be.

Her first single, 'Friday Dance Promenade/Damned ol' Dog', was released in December 1983, on Larry Wanagas' little Bumstead label. But it was her live performances which were getting her a reputation for being a l-l-l- ... little bit different, and when k.d. lang and her Reclines stole the show in 1984 at the prestigious Edmonton Folk Festival, there were plenty of music industry figures in the audience to witness her triumph and make a mental memo to themselves. In the end, though, it was someone who hadn't actually been at Edmonton who would snap up lang: Seymour Stein, boss of Warner Brothers' Sire label, the man who had previously snapped up Madonna.

One person who wasn't around to see his friend make such an impression was Drifter. Not long after he returned to Alberta, he was killed in a stupid fight at a party, which started with an argument about the music being played. But while one important man had gone from her life, another was just around the corner.

In 1985, lang and The Reclines were on a three-week tour of Japan, when she met another young Canadian, Ben Mink, then with the band Cano, and well-known for his skills as a violinist – and violin decorator. His customized fiddle was hollowed out and filled with little plastic and plaster figurines of animals and toys. He was obviously the man for k.d. lang – in more ways than one. 'His musicality, talent and attitude have anchored me, and made me more controlled', she said later. 'Without him, I'd be much more alternative and left-of-centre.'[13]

And, God knows, right from the onset of her career, she was considered a bit *too* alternative; she was an outsider, trying to get on the inside. It was always going to be a tough call, though talent and determination by the bucketful would take care of that. However, there was an additional factor which was always going to work against her – as far as the world outside Canada was concerned, anyway. The fact that she was from *inside* Canada – very *much* inside, indeed.

> 'The trouble with Canada, one of its prime ministers lamented, is that it has "too much geography and not enough history". And a standing joke among American publishers claims that the book title most guaranteed to ensure no sales whatsoever is Canada: Our Good Neighbor to the North'.[14]

Nearly ten years ago, MTV used to run a dopey game show called *Dead Or Canadian*. Contestants had to guess whether names they were given of obscure celebrities were either dead or ha-bloody-ha – just Canadian.

Perhaps you're one of the many people for whom the question 'name three famous Canadians' could be as tough as the old 'name three famous Belgians' poser? Right here are your starters for ten, then:

Which Canadian film director made the most successful movie ever? (Clue: it was a titanic bore.)

Which Canadian actor features in the top three best-paid in the world and was the star of the US box office smash of 1998? (Clue: he's rubber-faced and over-rated.)

Which Canadian singer was responsible for the biggest-ever selling album by a solo female singer?

(Clue: it just proved how many therapy-dependent, psycho-babblers there are in the world.)

Which other Canadian songstress sells an album every 1.2 seconds? (Clue: early in 1999, she said her career unlike her heart would not go on after 2000.)

(Answers at the end of the chapter.)

In many parts of the world outside Canada (and some inside), to be Canadian is not considered cool, which is ironic, given the country's famously long and severe winters. And, frankly, there are some parts of Canada that can be distinctly uncool.

Over the last decade, Canadian Customs have made a nasty habit of seizing and banning lesbian and gay books, especially those ordered by a bookshop in k.d. lang's backyard, Little Sisters Book and Art Emporium in Vancouver. Pat Califia's controversial *Macho Sluts* has been a particular favourite – banned in Canada (and then the ban rescinded) no less than five times. A whole clutch of established lesbian and gay authors have had titles nixed, including Oscar Wilde, John Preston, David Leavitt, Dorothy Allison and David Wojnarowicz. Then there were the books which have, in a rush of homosexual panic, been misidentified as gay, and banned anyway: *Hot Hotter Hottest* wasn't a book about gay guys with a certain horse-like quality, but merely a book of chilli pepper recipes.

And, lest we forget, it was Toronto Canada's cultural capital where Madonna, in the middle of her 1990 *Blonde Ambition* tour, was threatened with arrest for indecency if she touched her crotch during any of the numbers. The police claimed they were only 'acting on complaints from the public'.

Yet Toronto's annual Pride festival is the biggest free lesbian and gay event in the world, the country's first female mayor was a dyke and it has some of the best anti-discriminatory legislation anywhere in the free world.

Unlike compatriots Joni Mitchell and Alanis Morissette, k.d. lang didn't head South to become an honorary California girl. Even Quebec-born Celine Dion, currently the biggest selling solo artist in the world, jokes that if you cut her, she might bleed maple syrup. (Dollars, more like.)

lang stayed put, in unfashionable Alberta, and resolutely refused to dye her roots to match the star-spangled banner. 'Being Canadian is a nice balance between America and Europe', she once said.[15] 'I'm also alternative because of Canada, there's something romantic about being Canadian. We're a relatively unpopulated, somewhat civilized and clean and resourceful country'.[16] What a pity most of America and Europe don't seem to think so.

In a 1998 supplement, *Empire* magazine sniffed, 'Cliff Thorburn. Maple syrup. "Mounted" police. Most Canadian exports are as dull as dishwater.' Even in the midst of a lang-friendly feature, *Rolling Stone* writer Mim Udovitch couldn't stop herself having a dig: 'The cultural presumption against lesbians, feminists, vegetarians and Canadians having senses of humour is really pretty strong (and with Canadians the culture might have a point).'[17]

A point undoubtedly appreciated by the creators of, and thousands of visitors to, the Anti-Canada Website. Yes, there really is one. It has a list of 'Evil Canadians', and a page of 'Canadian Jokes'. But all you humourless Canucks shouldn't take umbrage – the site's managers are adamant it was 'designed as a joke, and should be taken as such. It is SATIRE!'. So, 'don't send any hate mail'. Good joke, isn't it?

And now just think how funny you'd find it – especially if you're reading this in Ireland – if it was called the 'Anti-Irish Website', with a page for 'Irish Jokes' and a list of 'Evil Irish' ...

Canadian identity seems to be something its native performers can choose to abandon or keep at will. Alanis Morissette was a child star at 11 in her homeland, until at 16 she decamped from Ottawa to LA, and came on like a US-style rock chick, *à la* Sheryl Crow et al., yowling out her clumpy rock songs about dismal relationships. But the image and the songs did the trick: to date, *Jagged Little Pill* has sold 28 million copies worldwide, the biggest-selling album by a female solo artist, ever. Journalist Sheryl Garratt observed that it was probably Morissette's 'very blandness that made her so accessible'.[18] Sticking firmly in the 'cock-rock-with-female-vocals' genre and singing about giving her guy some unusual interval refreshments in a theatre probably helped as well. The huge AOR market remains the mainstay of the American music industry, and Morissette slipped right into the mass sales groove.

Whereas a defiantly proud Canadian, lesbian, country-rocker turned torch singer, unfettered by a 'victim' mantle, with all her diversity, her purity of voice, was never going to be in the same league. 'I was one of the first Canadians to come out of the West, have international success and really focus on my roots', lang said.[19]

Of course, lang's relationship with her home town and country has fluxed and changed. During the early years of her career, she was the Alberta Rose, the pride of Consort, which proudly dubbed itself, 'k.d. lang country'. In 1988, came what she always describes as 'one of the greatest moments of my career': performing 'Turn Me Round' live at the opening ceremony of the Winter Olympics in Calgary, while hundreds of ice dancers, skiers and Mounties frolicked around her.

Nothing, it seemed, could threaten the love Alberta had for its favourite daughter – nothing, except her love for all creatures great and small, a view not generally held by the vast majority of her countrymen and -women whose take on animals: that you shoot 'em, stuff 'em or eat 'em.

As has been documented till the cows come home – unless they're in Canada, in which case they don't – lang agreed to make a TV commercial for the international animal rights group PETA (People for Ethical Treatment of Animals), also beloved by the likes of Chrissie Hynde. Broadcast in June 1990, it seemed innocuous enough, by today's standards – lang cuddled a cow and said, 'I'm from cattle country and that's why I became a vegetarian. Meat stinks, and not just for animals, but for human health and the environment.'

THE INTERESTING NEW ADDITION TO THE 'HOME OF K.D. LANG' SIGN

In just a few minutes, it was done – lang, in her own words, went 'from being Canada's little queen to all of a sudden having the whole country against me'. Given that Alberta is Canada's biggest beef-producing province, the response to the PETA ad was hardly surprising. But it is amusing, though, to observe that she caused more offence in her homeland by coming out so strongly in favour of animal rights than ... coming out – although a little homophobia was, ahem, in evidence when the 'entering Consort, 'home of k.d. lang' sign suddenly sported an unusual new phrase of welcome: 'Eat Beef Dyke'.

lang received some words of wisdom from another 'originally-from-Canada' artist who knew whereof she spoke, Joni Mitchell, who warned her, 'In Canada they eat their young'.

Of course, k.d. lang was not the only lesbian artist to ruffle feathers by appearing in a PETA ad: in 1995, Melissa Etheridge and her partner Julie Cypher were pictured nude on a poster for the organization's 'I'd rather go naked than wear fur' campaign.

Etheridge then found herself the target of fierce criticism – not from outraged American fur-farmers but, incredibly, AIDS activists and researchers who found her alliance with a pressure group that opposed animal testing for medical purposes abhorrent. The pressure took its toll: Etheridge asked for the poster to be withdrawn and did no more high-profile publicity for PETA.

So then – it's not just Canadians that 'eat their young'.

(Answers: James Cameron, Jim Carrey, Alanis Morissette, Celine Dion)

ANGEL WITH A LARIAT, K.D. LANG AND THE RECLINES' FIRST ALBUM

A truly western experience

Just as The Pogues took traditional Irish music and fused it with punk energy, so did k.d. lang with country music: 'I was a woman who had the attitude of a young eighties woman who had been influenced by the Sex Pistols, whoever ...'[20] Coupled with the Eastern European influences and customized fiddling of the man she called 'her creative husband', Ben Mink, she challenged the conventional wisdom that says 'if it ain't from the South, it ain't country.' 'Country', she patiently explained, 'is a conglomeration of European music, Mexican music, Irish fiddle tunes, Slavic polkas – Canadians have those same influences as well.'[21] With her ancestry a mixture of Dutch, Scottish, English, Icelandic, German-Jewish and Cree Indian, lang was living proof of diverse cultural influences – the Alberta Rose was very much a hybrid.

And, never mind how sincere all that stuff about Patsy Cline was – this particular musical genre was chosen because it suited her purposes, as she later admitted: 'Country was a way for me to incorporate punk, and was a good way for me to sing, because country puts the vocalist up front. It suits my voice, but it also let me be really energetic.'[22] It was amusing to see those punk influences let loose again, albeit briefly, a few times during her 1996 tour, when she turned 'If I Were You' into a not-unconvincing piece of grunge rock. It was almost as if having Ozzy Osbourne's former guitarist in her band had suddenly gone to her head.

The first glimmers of Patsy Cline came when she was at Red Deer College in 1982, playing what she calls 'a Patsy Cline-like character' in a show called *Country Corral*, about a young woman who dreams of being her favourite singer. Apparently, she'd never heard of Patsy Cline at that point, but that's who she ended up modelling her stage persona on. Then she was given a couple of Cline's LPs for her 21st birthday, and also remembered the recurring dreams about plane crashes she'd had throughout most of her childhood.

'One night', she recalled, 'I got her records and was smoking dope and got this vision of what I was and what I wanted to do.'[23] The vision was of a young woman with a short haircut, wearing sawn-off cowboy boots, and grab-bag skirts and fringed shirts in clashing colours, fronting a band called The Reclines. And thus began what she called her 'seven-year rampage through country music'.[24]

The 'rampage' would involve her image to almost a greater degree than her music. 'The look changes with the kind of music I'm doing',[25] she observed. During her country and western years, that 'look' came mostly from rummaging around Salvation Army and Value Village stores. *Billboard's* country correspondence decided her outfits looked like they had 'been on loan for a decade from the Roy Rogers Museum, and the nearest Goodwill store'.[26] Once she had signed for Warner Bros, an early, and wise, decision was taken by Carl Scott in the company' s marketing department to get their new girl as many TV appearances as possible, so audiences would get used to the way she looked.

Musically, the first album in the rampage, *A Truly Western Experience*, released on Larry Wanagas' Bumstead Records in 1984, was rough, ready and raunchy, with no more than a good old-fashioned, basic country-rock instrumentation from the first Reclines line-up, who were yet to be dressed in Mink. But it did serve as a useful extended demo, and to this extent, it served its purpose: it showed off the voice, the energy and the irony. Oh, and of course, there was the image: the long crew cut, the ill-fitting skirt, the thick glasses and the childlike, cut-and-paste collage artwork, complete with a picture of Patsy Cline.

It also hinted of other things that were a little bit different: on some of the tracks, she sounded like a cross between early Elvis and Jerry Lee Lewis. True, she did a version of the country classic 'There He Goes', but changed the lyrics to the non-gender specific 'There You Go'.

The self-penned 'Pine And Stew' contains one of the unlikeliest lyrics heard in a country song: 'Do you think I'm mental?' And on the album's final track, 'Hooked On Junk', Drifter's paeon to grungers, she sounds like Kurt Cobain unplugged, with just a hint of her performance art days thrown in towards the end. For *Angel With A Lariat*, the first album for Warner Bros in 1987, lang and the Reclines were put together with a 'name' producer: twangy guitarists Dave Edmunds, front man of rockabilly 'supergroup' Rockpile, which also included legendary producer Nick Lowe. As well as enjoying sporadic success with Rockpile and as a solo artist, Edmunds spent much of the early eighties behind the console, twiddling the knobs for Carl Perkins, retro rockabillies The Stray Cats on their first two albums, and the Everly Brothers on their comeback album, *EB '84*. However, the word was, Edmunds wasn't exactly keen to do the honours on *Lariat*. They were given a month to record the album, which was done in London in June 1986 and, by all accounts, it was not the most enjoyable time either party had spent in the studio. lang's insistence on recording her vocals live and using a hand-held microphone to do so were rumoured to have driven her producer up the wall.

Lariat included 'High Time For A Detour', the first song she and Mink wrote together. There were also three songs she'd penned solo: 'Diet Of Strange Places', which gave more than a little nod in the direction of the beloved Patsy, and an early mention of 'craving', a recurring theme; 'Angel With A Lariat', with its fifties-style, ooh-ah-ooh-ah close harmonies on the chorus; and the unremarkable 'Pay Dirt'.

Lariat sounds unmistakably like a Dave Edmunds album – as ever, the twang's the thang that stands out. Trouble is, it should have been lang's voice doing that. On 'Three Cigarettes In An Ashtray', her voice is mixed gossamer-thin, valiantly but vainly doing battle with Anne Dudley's lush string arrangement. Elsewhere, there was, she later complained, 'Tons and tons of reverb, 150 milliseconds on everything'.[27] 'Watch Your Step Polka' was little more than a chance for the Reclines to show off what a great band they were, with just faint traces of their lead vocalist.

The pairing of lang and Edmunds was no marriage made in heaven, musically or personally. 'I was far too immature to really know what the hell was going on', she said later. 'I hated it.'[28] she admitted 'I was over-emotional because I was 23 and wanted to be star.'[29] (actually, she was 25).

One of her early publicists once told a journalist that they had 'loathed her – she was rude, obnoxious, and incredibly demanding for someone who had been in the business for five minutes'.[30] It's true, you do get a hint of this in her early TV performances – she's a crazy cowpunk bursting with energy, totally hyper, knocking over everything with that big voice and that unsubtle image. She can see stardom, and she's going for it.

The barnstorming lang/Edmunds treatment of Lynn Anderson's originally more delicate 'Rose Garden' ensured the single was a radio hit, if nothing else, especially in the UK. DJs started to get their tongues around 'k.d. lang', and some closet country fans wanted to find out more about this singer who was obviously a l-l-l … little bit different.

Hearing it bouncing and crashing its way out of the radio for the first time, you couldn't help but sit up and take notice.

Who the hell was this cowgirl? And so you'd go down to the record shop, and flick through the L–Ms in the country album section – it was all in vinyl in those days, of course – and, sure enough, there was Angel With A Lariat. *And there she was on the front cover, the centrepiece of a framed picture, surrounded by little plastic toys and animals that looked like they'd dropped out of Ben Mink's customized violin.*

And look at that short hair! Sure, she's wearing a frock, but it's not what you'd call a girly frock.

Now, who's this guy on the back cover, wearing that ill-fitting cowboy outfit, posing for the photo like he's the one who's going to ride off into the sunset with the girl. It's not Dave Edmunds, is it?

Hang on, it can't be … it is, it's her! But look at her – she's decked out in full cowboy drag. She looks like she's auditioning for the lesbian version of Village

*People. It's so butch, it' s enough to make your eyes water. And look at the inside
sleeve get that "how about it, girls?" expression, and that short feather-cut. Does
she know what she's doing? Oh, come off it, of course she must ... but does anyone
else? How did she get away with it? How will she get away with it?*

The odd critic also seemed aware that something unusual was afoot and it
wasn't twelve inches. Q's David Sinclair declared *Lariat* 'remarkable for its
high energy approach to a typically languid genre' and mused, 'Colonial
country punks, whatever next?' On the strength of the album, backed up by a
hectic schedule of concerts and TV appearances, she won the Canadian
Country Music Association Entertainer of the Year and Rising New Star
awards, and was already being hailed by some critics as 'a scintillating
combination of space cadet, macho woman, serious philosopher, caring
human and one hell of an engaging talent'.[31]

But most of the wider world – and especially Nashville – wasn't paying much
attention to *Lariat* or lang. So what did Little Miss Showoff do next? Why,
something guaranteed to make them do just that, of course.

★ ★ ★ ★ ★ ★

k.d. lang was leaving her Reclines behind and heading for the heartland of
country, Tennessee, for a date with a man who was one of the main pillars in
the house of country. Mary Martin of RCA Records was the matchmaker,
and lang's date was with none other than Owen Bradley, Mr Country
himself, the legendary producer on most of Patsy Cline' s recordings.

It was not unknown for some uppity young singer to waltz into Nashville
country, team up with one of its top-drawer producers and try to prove that
they were a 'real' singer, able to genre-jump their way to mainstream respect.

Which is exactly what Elvis Costello tried to do. In 1981, he took a sharp
right-turn away from rock and ambled into Nashville with his Attractions to
make a country album, *Almost Blue*, with Billy Sherrill, Tammy Wynette's
producer. Almost blue? It was almost total disaster. Costello's fanbase wasn't

ready for such a dramatic and, at the time, unfashionable musical switch, and Nashville sure as hell wasn't ready to embrace a former punk with, as they saw it, musical pretensions way beyond the capabilities of him and his band. In a British television documentary made during the recording of the album, one of the Attractions was heard murmuring about Sherrill, 'He thinks we're crap'.

Well, chaps, in country terms, you were. But k.d. lang wasn't.

Owen Bradley was virtually retired, and suffering health problems. But he had been impressed by lang's rendition of 'Three Cigarettes In An Ashtray' on *The Johnny Carson Show*. It took a few approaches to coax Bradley back into the studio but, once the decision was made, there were to be no half-measures: he enlisted the services of many of the musicians who had also worked with him and Cline and, on half of the tracks, lang's vocals were supported by The Jordanaires, who had performed the same duties for Presley.

To the country establishment, it looked like nothing more than a cynical attempt to ride on Patsy Cline's coat-tails. But lang's approach was full of respect for the man she was working with, and for the other country legends who, in agreeing to appear on the album, were 'embracing this young upstart'. This 'embrace' came with the record's final track, 'Honky Tonk Angels Medley' – comprising the classics, 'In The Evening', 'You Nearly Lose Your Mind' and 'Blues Stay Away From Me' – where lang was joined on vocals by three other Nashville legends, Kitty Wells, Loretta Lynn and Brenda Lee.

Shadowland was a showcase for k.d. lang the singer, rather than k.d. lang the songwriter: there were no self-compositions this time, just a thoughtfully chosen selection of new and old country songs. With Bradley's production – a darn sight more empathic than Dave Edmunds' reverb-heavy efforts on *Lariat* – she was able to demonstrate to any sceptics both her respect for the traditional material and her ability to meet its vocal demands. Many pundits still consider the album to be her finest recorded vocal work, and they're not far off the mark.

The opening track, Chris Isaak's 'Western Stars', was a dreamy beginning, with a soft Tex-Mex arrangement, and the 'young upstart' performing vocal gymnastics up and down the scales, continuing in a similar vein on 'Lock, Stock And Teardrops', with its tinkly Cline-like piano riffs. The echoes of Cline were at their strongest on the weepy 'I Wish I Didn't Love You So' and 'Tears Don't Care Who Cries Them'. Another tearjerker, 'I'm Down To My Last Cigarette', was performed against a nicely contrasting, jaunty arrangement. '(Waltz Me) Once Again Around The Dance Floor', 'Sugar Moon' and 'Don't Let The Stars Get In Your Eyes' were singalong favourites, full of charm. 'Busy Being Blue' and 'Black Coffee' both benefited from soft jazz makeovers, and bore signs of what was to come with *Ingenue* and *Drag*. But it was the title track that really showed why Bradley had agreed to work with lang: sliding all over the octaves and key shifts, it's a phenomenally tricky song to sing, but she made it sound wickedly simple.

Unusually for a producer, Bradley's name featured as prominently on the album's packaging as its singer. It was sub-titled *The Owen Bradley Sessions* on the cover, which also featured inner sleeve notes written by Bradley for his new Western star, accompanied by photos of the artist with her producer.

Linking up with Bradley was an audacious and risky move, but it paid off – in spades. *Shadowland* spent more than 30 weeks on the *Cashbox Country* album charts, taking its time to climb from a modest 43 to its peak in the no. 5 slot. The album spent 121 weeks on *Billboard's* Country Album charts and even produced a couple of minor hit singles. In Canada, she waltzed off with a Juno and two Canadian Country Music Association awards, and then topped this with three Grammy nominations. Ten years on, her vocals on *Shadowland* still sound like the work of an artist of maturity – anyone who could work their way round the major and minor twists and turns of the title track itself didn't really have to do anything else to prove their sheer quality and class.

And, more significantly, it proved, again, that if a singer could persuade one musical legend to work with them – however reluctant they might be at first – others might just do the same. Shortly before she began work on *Shadowland*, Roy Orbison, working on the soundtrack of a duff movie called *Hiding Out*, agreed to duet with her on a new version of his classic ballad,

'Crying'. This recording, almost more than any other she was to do, gifted her a lifelong musical legacy, and paved the way to genuine stardom.

It brought her her first Grammy nomination, for Best Country Music Collaboration (along with the 'Honky Tonk Angels Medley') and, in Canada, the Juno for Female Vocalist of the Year. It was re-released as a single in the UK in 1993, reaching no. 13 – her biggest singles' chart showing to date.

But, as everyone recognized at the time, and in hindsight, the real breakthrough provided by her link with Orbison and this particular song was her performance of it in May 1989, at New York's Radio City Hall for the Songwriters' Hall of Fame show, which was paying posthumous tribute to Orbison who had died in December 1988. Her breathtaking performance of it brought the audience to its feet, giving her a spontaneous, show-stopping ovation. Orbison's widow, Barbara, regarded it as the defining moment in lang's career, the point where she 'reached star quality'.

This working-with-musical-legends stuff was having the desired effect ....

But, for what was to signal the end of her 'rampage through country', lang opted for a less legendary approach. In 1989, she returned to Vancouver, had a fruitful songwriting session with Ben Mink, gathered her trusty Reclines together and set about recording *Absolute Torch And Twang*. It was the album that sealed the lang/Mink songwriting partnership, though it did include covers of the defiantly large 'Big, Big Love', the jaunty 'Full Moon Of Love' and the Willie Nelson/Faron Young-penned 'Three Days', with its walking bassline and lang sounding for all the world like a swinging young Elvis – and yes, it *was* beautiful.

The jaunty, tongue-in-cheek 'Big Boned Gal' was the perfect good-humoured response to all the old insecurities and negativity about her tall, strong physique, while 'Wallflower Waltz' was a sadder reflection on the same theme. She and Mink mixed up their rock and country with the more upbeat 'Didn't I' and 'Walkin' In And Out Of Your Arms', and her solo-penned 'Nowhere To Stand' was lang in rare social commentary mode, delivering a moving, remarkably unpolemical indictment of child abuse. Most significantly, two lang/Mink songs on this album clearly pointed the way to *Ingenue*: the touchingly plaintive 'Trail Of Broken Hearts', and the bluesy 'Pullin' Back The Reins' which, despite its obvious lyrical country and western metaphors, was just a spark away from being a full-blown torch song.

Two singles from the album dented the lower regions of *Billboard's* country charts, 'Down To My Last Cigarette' (no. 21) and 'Full Moon Of Love' (no. 22). Bolstered by a 14 month-long worldwide tour, *Absolute Torch And Twang* sold over a million copies in America and spent an incredible 104 weeks on *Billboard's* country charts, even more remarkable, when you realize it was achieved with virtually no airplay on any country stations. It even spent over a year in the national pop album charts. When the album went gold in 1990, lang issued a sarcastic press release: 'Me and Metallica ... gold, with no radio!' And the sarcasm was vindicated, turning to sweet revenge, when she waltzed off with the 1990 Grammy award for Best Female Country Vocalist.

But, by then, even the industry pundits were expressing a little embarrassment at the not-too-subtle discriminatory treatment of some of the biggest 'new country' artists, including lang and Lyle Lovett: *Billboard* went so far as to run a story, headlined 'Country PDs [Programme Directors] Resist Grammy Winners', which provided proof positive what lang had long suspected. Bruce Sharman, Programme Director of WSM-FM Nashville, with power of his station's playlists, said: 'I think lang and Lovett are both tremendous artists. I appreciate what they do; I'm just not sure that a majority of the public does.'[32] Mark Lewis from Wisconsin station WYNE Appleton pointed the finger of guilt at lang's image: 'I was watching the Grammys in a little hick bar, and you could see the cross-section of people. There was a couple that were clearly our listeners and they cheered when lang won. But there were also two guys at the other end of the bar asking if that was a guy or a girl on the screen.'[33] Nick Hunter, in charge of Warner's national country sales and promotion, reluctantly agreed with Sharman's view: '... the image lang projects scares the living hell out of country radio, she doesn't look like the rest of them and that intimidates people.'[34]

It's an understatement that this was all frustrating and vexing, to both lang and her label, but she had, when all is said and done, gained precisely what she had set out to from country music. After *Ingenue* was released in 1992, she admitted to a journalist 'I used the country music industry to become a successful singer while being alternative'. Country music had not, after all, been an early major influence on her music, as she later acknowledged: 'I probably listen to the jazz singers and cabaret music – the Cole Porter stuff and Peggy Lee – as much if not more than I ever listened to country'.[35] Indeed, these influences can clearly be heard on some of the tracks on *Shadowland*, several years before her country excursion came to an end. However, even after she'd hung up her rhinestones for good, she still maintained she was 'a hundred per cent' serious about her Patsy Cline obsession.

A Canadian woman launching a radical image and musical assault on such a traditionally conservative musical genre was always going to be tricky, at best. And, of course, claiming to be the living reincarnation of one of country's legends was never likely to endear her to its establishment. And, apart from her image, there were plenty of other differences to ensure Nashville would never really want to claim her as their own. One incident, recalled by an anonymous C&W pundit, seemed to symbolize the culture clash: lang was appearing on a Brenda Lee TV special when, at the end of the show, 'America The Beautiful' was played and audience and performers all stood as one. Except one didn't. 'k.d. didn't stand up. She was the only one ... y' know, you'd have to be a Communist not to stand up'.[36]

Or, perhaps, just a Canadian ...

In the late eighties and early nineties, there was much hyped-up talk about 'new country' – and, especially, 'new women in country', spearheaded by the likes of Nanci Griffith and Mary-Chapin Carpenter, superb songwriters both. Neither Griffith's or Carpenter's attitudes, expressed in their lyrics, could be said to be in the tradition of the stereotypical long-suffering, wronged country women, *à la* Wynette or Cline. But their images, while light on the rhinestoned frocks and bouffant wigs, have hardly been threatening, and they convey nothing which even hints at sexual ambiguity. And it's worth remembering that Griffith's and Carpenter's songs get covered a lot by other singers; k.d. lang's still don't and never have. Coincidence – or is it just that they're better songwriters? Adam Sweeting of *The Guardian* saw it rather differently: 'It's obvious why Nashville couldn't cope with lang. She's too clever, too powerful and too ironic.'[37]

Despite all the talk about 'new country', the American country audience and establishment, with its roots planted deep in Southern soil, will always prefer its main female players to be more traditionally homespun and, dare it be said, not too cosmopolitan. After all, the biggest selling female country artist of all time is not to be found amongst the internationally-popular Wynettes or Partons (who is, after all, a bit too Hollywood nowadays) – in fact, it's Reba McEntire, the former housewife who hails from Oklahoma, and has managed to notch up 40 million album sales in the last 20 years, without the need to tour the UK or Europe once, prior to her 1999 tour in those territories.

Of course, not all of the country establishment, past and present, regarded lang, though Reba-negative, as a bad thing. One of her Nashville heroines, Minnie Pearl, said, just a tad wistfully, 'She represents the freedom we wish we all had'.[38] And persuading Owen Bradley, Mr Nashville himself, to come out of retirement, and getting Lynn (Patsy Cline's best friend), Lee and Wells to take part in a country gals-singalong hardly indicates total rejection.

But it was hard to ignore some home truths: despite all the awards festooned on her outside of Nashville, k.d. lang never got a single Country Music Association nomination. Not one. It was the clearest message Nashville, and the values it represented, could send her – a kind of 'we don't serve your kind in this town, stranger' message.

The 1989–90 *Torch And Twang* global jaunt, which wound up with three nights in London, was a *tour de force*. It firmly established her, once and for all, as an exceptional live performer, which critics were not slow to acknowledge: 'Not many country singers have such a self-deprecating sense of humour, or obviously enjoy themselves so much on stage, and there are none who can match such quirky antics with the ability to display quite unexpected emotion, power and intensity.'[39]

But by then, she'd had enough of waiting for Nashville's seal of approval – she decided to hang up her cowboy boots for good.She took a break from performing, and prepared to make her feature film-acting debut, in Percy Adlon's *Salmonberries*, which would call for her to play a young, confused, truculent woman from a small, remote town, who falls in love with an unobtainable woman.

It was a role that could have served as a rehearsal for what was about to engulf her offscreen.

Craving it, getting it

In the panic that gripped the American entertainment business – especially Hollywood – in the years immediately following Rock Hudson's death from AIDS in 1985, male stars were not exactly queueing up to be campaigning and fundraising figureheads. Virtually from the time when the epidemic started to cut a swathe through America and, to a slightly lesser extent, Britain, female entertainers led the way: the names of Elizabeth Taylor, Bette Midler, Liza Minnelli, Madonna and Shirley Maclaine spring to mind, and it was Joan Rivers who was the first major US entertainer to do AIDS benefits – under threats of death made to her and her family.

A good number have stayed the course for the cause, and, of course, k.d. lang is amongst them. Her public involvement began with an ambitious charity project that was full of good intentions but, through no fault of its own, suffered from the fact that, in 1990, AIDS was not a 'fashionable' cause, especially in the mainstream music industry.

Red, Hot And Blue was the brainchild of two friends, Leigh Blake, a London-based film-maker, and John Carlin, a New York-based writer and lawyer, conceived as a ninety-minute global TV and music event produced by Initial Film and Television, that would bring together some of the biggest names in contemporary music and film 'to help focus attention on the AIDS tragedy and to affirm our power to make a difference'.

The TV special would be shown in as many countries as would take it, on the 1990 World AIDS Day, December 1. Shortly after, Chrysalis records would release the album/CD, BMG Video, a tape of the programme, and all proceeds would be distributed by the non–profit-making organization King Cole, Inc., to AIDS charities around the world.

THE COVER OF THE RED HOT AND BLUE VIDEO FOR WHICH
K.D. SANG 'SO IN LOVE'

The concept was that each artist, working with a film or video director, would produce their own visual and musical interpretation of a Cole Porter song of their choice. Porter's songs were chosen, according to Blake and Carlin, 'because of their undeniable artistry and cross-generational appeal as well as the music's overall affirmation of love and social experimentation ... Cole Porter's songs ... are about romance with intelligence. We're not telling people not to make love, we're telling them to be smart about it.'

There were some impressive names amongst the roster of directors who supported the project: Jim Jarmusch, Derek Jarman, Percy Adlon, Jonathan Demme, Stephen Frears and Neil Jordan. However, the list did not include any of Hollywood's major players: there were to be no Spielbergs or Coppolas or Scorceses. Similarly, the list of musical artists agreeing to participate was impressive enough – Sinead O'Connor, Annie Lennox, U2, Neneh Cherry, Erasure, Tom Waits – but, at this point in the history of AIDS, no Madonna or George Michael or Elton John or David Bowie or Queen would be volunteering their services.

German director Percy Adlon, still best known for *Bagdad Café*, was one of lang's favourites and happily agreed to work with her on *Red, Hot And Blue*. For her contribution, she had originally chosen 'I Am In Love', from the 1953 musical *Can-Can*. This would have been interesting if it had been done with the introductory verse, that began 'Sit down, mad'moiselle'. But, at Adlon's suggestion, she eventually plumped for 'So In Love', from the 1948 musical *Kiss Me Kate*, although they jettisoned Adlon's original concept of her weeping all the way through the song. In hindsight, of course, lang's version of the Porter classic was a signpost of a musical metamorphosis to come. Her interpretation of this bittersweet *crie-de-coeur* was recorded before she lost her heart to *Ingenue*'s inspiration, but her vocal emoting is convincing enough to convey the desperation and devotion of someone hopelessly in love. Indeed, it would not have sounded out of place on her next album.

But it was the song's video that was the real landmark. A disconsolate lang is shown in an apartment, doing some laundry, taking care to boil a woman's slip. This is intercut with images that show someone's been seriously ill: a drip, a hospital light, an invalid's shower–chair. You could think it's a friend or relative of hers who's died – until towards the end when she hangs the slip up to dry, and tenderly runs her face and hands over it, before slumping down and wrenching the song's finale out of her vocal chords. Then you know it's her girlfriend who was the patient. Simple, effective and quite remarkable.

In a climate which was barely acknowledging that women were as much at risk as anyone else, and that there might be safer sex issues for lesbians, here was k.d. lang saying, hey, all you dykes, we can get it too. 'It's important to me to let people know that women get AIDS too, that it's not just a gay male disease', she said.[40] It went against the view then taken by many lesbian communities the world over, which were trying to deny that most women had once had an active heterosexual love life – never mind the touchy subject of active and current bisexuality – and that lesbianism didn't work as a retrospective vaccine against STDs.

Even viewed nearly a decade on, the video remains startling in the explicitness of its message and the sense of loss expressed so simply but powerfully. In as much as pop videos can be claimed to be 'important', this understated, underappreciated gem was one of the most important.

However, the ambitious and worthy project it was made for ran into problems. Scott Millaney, one of *Red, Hot And Blue*'s executive producers admitted that they had 'encountered considerable prejudice towards the project because of the underlying message of AIDS'. In England, the project couldn't get the BBC to agree to transmit the programme. Eventually, Channel Four – then Britain's least-viewed channel – agreed to take it and it was duly broadcast on December 1 1990.

The programme received scant press coverage, its worthy educational messages – especially k.d. lang's – largely ignored. Her video contribution and Jimmy Somerville's fell victim to American television censorship, being nipped and tucked to cleanse them of any overtly gay overtones. The album ended up a mish-mash of musical styles which the public didn't readily take to, and included a number of artists, such as the Thompson Twins, who were hardly commercial heavyweights at that point. It sold negligibly, and was sneered at by large sections of the music press. Steve Sutherland in *Melody Maker* said lang was amongst those who 'use their respective song simply to showcase their vocal talents'.[41]

But others were more positive: In *Sounds*, Damon Wise declared, 'Red Hot and Blue transcends the limitations of the [charity vinyl] genre with style and panache. No one ever advanced their careers by sticking up for "queers" and "junkies". Just think of those that didn't have the guts!'[42] Andrew Collins of *Vox* lauded the album as 'Special. Thrilling. Important. Inspired.'[43]

Despite a less than wholehearted welcome, The Red Hot Organization has continued to fight HIV and AIDS through popular culture. Since 1990, it has produced ten albums and related TV specials, raising over $6 million for AIDS relief in the process.

Adlon's cinematic muse had been Marianne Sagebrecht, for whom he had written quirky lead roles in *Sugarbaby* (1985), *Bagdad Café* (1988) and *Rosalie Goes Shopping* (1989). In 1990, Adlon started to dream up a role for the new woman in his creative life: and the woman he saw in his mind's eye was an androgynous-looking, sullen, inarticulate loner, without a father figure and longing for love with another woman.

Naturally, any resemblance between the *Salmonberries* character, Kotzebue, and any living person is coincidental – although it is amusing to note that the first time we see Kotz in the film, she's showing total and violent disrespect for books ...

Of course, being k.d. lang, the film had to involve something a tad unusual. For one thing, it meant she would have to read something other than a dictionary – a script. For another, here she was in her first film role, and what did it involve? Why, a nude scene – what else? The fact that the nudity was set in a North Alaskan library, of all places, and didn't actually involve sex was both very Adlon and *very* k.d. lang.

In *Salmonberries*, Adlon continued his cinematic preoccupation with pitching opposites against each other until they attracted, though not necessarily sexually. lang's dad Fred used to call her his 'boy-girl' and that's exactly what the role of the brooding Kotz was about - 'part-Eskimo, part-Canadian and part-k.d. lang, which is to say wholly unlike anyone else'.[44] Kotz's 'opposite' number is German migrant Roswitha (Rosel Zech), who runs the library in the small town after which Kotz is named. Like *Bagdad Café*, after an unpromising start, the two women form a close friendship in a harsh, claustrophobic environment, peopled by a motley bunch of eccentrics. However, this time, Adlon introduced a sexual element into the relationship, with Kotz falling in love with Roswitha and attempting to make love with her when they visit Berlin together, to exorcise Roswitha's Iron Curtain demons.

The film was shot partly in Berlin, but mostly in an extremely cold and remote part of Alaska, 400 miles from Anchorage, and only accessible by snowmobile, boat or plane. During the Berlin shoot, lang and Ben Mink took time out to visit areas of Poland which featured in his family's history.

Unfortunately, Adlon's quirky brand of magic failed to work with *Salmonberries*. There was no real on-screen chemistry between his two leading ladies – the pivotal scene in which they argue after Kotz's Skidoo blows up, leaving them stranded in the middle of a frozen wasteland, showed this up hideously well – and even the minor characters failed to engage you as they had in his previous films. It suffered from some of the worst pretensions which independent European films are occasionally guilty of, including 'symbolic' dreamlike scenes, which verged on self-parody.

Moreover, many gay audiences felt frustrated with the decision to deny the two lead characters any sexual bonding. After its UK release in April 1992, *Salmonberries* was attacked by some of the gay press precisely because of this. However, lang herself rebuffed this sort of criticism, saying that allowing the relationship to develop into a sexual one would have made it 'a real lesbian film. And what good is that? Then people would think you're just being trendy or you're trying to sell the film through controversy.'[45]

As if appearing nude in your first film role wasn't going to 'sell the film through controversy' ...

Not surprisingly, this most foreign of foreign films had a hard time finding a US distributor. It won the Grand Prix at the 1991 Montreal Film Festival, but that was about it, as far as getting plaudits went. When it was finally released in America in 1994, it featured in many critics' choices of worst films of the year. Mick LaSalle of the *San Francisco Chronicle* found it 'earnestly awful ... the film was all talk – boring talk'.[46] UK critics were no kinder: 'An exhaustingly slow-moving tale which makes for trying viewing, this has two frustrating central characters coming across as completely unsympathetic and self-obsessed' and advised kd, on the strength of her 'hopeless performance ... would be well-advised not to pack in the day job just yet'.[47]

lang admitted that acting had been 'a little bit addictive'; 'It's not my first love, but it's sure something I'd like to have an affair with.'[48] But her 'day job' was about to take over, 24:7, with no breaks.

★ ★ ★ ★ ★ ★

Apart from her voice, k.d. lang's square-peg attitude is what marks her out as just so much more interesting than your usual conveyor-belt popster.

However, the oddest of all her oddities has to be her own admission that she didn't fall truly, madly, deeply in love until she was 30. That's three-oh, 30. Now, that *is* odd. Still, given that it resulted in one of the all-time great albums about unrequited love, it was definitely worth the wait.

Prior to making the album, lang and Mink hadn't got around to speaking to each other for months, and it wasn't certain he would want to travel in the musical direction she was headed for. However, they did begin writing new songs together in January 1991 and then, whoosh – there went her heart – but back came the new album.

By a strange coincidence, lang losing her heart to mystery woman Ms X nearly coincided with her temporarily losing her perfect pitch. She suddenly found she was singing flat, and consulted masseuses, homeopaths and vocal specialists – all to no avail. It was only when she went to her dentist that the root of the problem lay in ... just that: an infected root canal, which was pushing on her right Eustachian tube. Coincidental – or, possibly, a physical manifestation of her loss of emotional control? It's one for the shrinks.

1992's *Ingenue* has been called many things in its time – the ultimate emotional masochist's album being just one of them. But what was especially significant about the album was that it marked the perfect meeting of musical minds between lang and Ben Mink. Not for nothing has it been observed that Mink has been to lang what Nelson Riddle was to Sinatra. Every great singer, no matter how great, needs an empathic musical collaborator, be they a songwriting partner, an arranger or producer. lang was exceptionally fortunate that she found all three in one person – and had the wisdom to recognize it. *Ingenue* would not only be k.d. lang's finest hour, but Mink's as well.

The ten-song cycle that became *Ingenue* is, musically and lyrically, one of the most eloquent expressions in popular music of the emotional three-ring circus that we endure when we fall in love with the wrong person. The 1990 cover of 'So In Love' for the *Red, Hot and Blue* project was almost a dress rehearsal for the raw emotional unburdening that was to manifest itself a few years later: the near-masochistic love for a beloved who, for one reason or another, can't return the feelings.

You know how it goes – one day, life is just bumbling along quite normally; then, without warning, you see a face across a room, or a street, or an office, and suddenly, there go your heart, your control and your life, out of the window, gone for the duration. And there's not a damn thing you can do about it. You have to wait for the illness to pass; like a virus, it has to run its course, and no remedy in a packet or a bottle is really going to do any good. You just have to feel it – until you don't feel it anymore.

And lang was, as she expressed in 'The Mind Of Love', talking to herself, concerned for her health and wondering what the hell was going on in her head. Save me, she pleaded, wash me clean, I'm raw, outside myself, I've been poisoned by a thing of might and dread. And there must be a reason for it – mustn't there?

Initially, of course, the realization that you've completely lost it over someone brings a heady rush of temporary joy and *Ingenue*'s moment of blissfulness was 'Miss Chatelaine', written when, as lang said, she 'felt like Doris Day holidaying in Paris'.[49] The blurred photographs of lang that adorned the cover of *Ingenue* told the story almost as well as the songs it contained: blurred, sepia images of a face full of pain and contemplation, that refuses to look the camera in the eye.

Ingenue had it all: the Riddle-esque string arrangements by Ben Mink, highly congenial production by him, lang and Greg Penny, and the most eloquent and least-mannered vocal performances of her career to date. And the songs, the songs ...

There's the gentle samba of 'Still Thrives This Love', peppered with echoes of Eastern European musical influences and Mink's own roots. On 'Miss Chatelaine', the album's only truly joyous moment, lang does indeed sound like she's filled with the spirit of Doris Day skipping through the Tuileries, or shouting out her secret love from the top of the Eiffel Tower. In complete contrast, 'Wash Me Clean' drips with the sheer agony and humiliation of loving someone who can't, or won't, love you back, while 'Save Me' and 'So It Shall Be' are slightly more dignified pleas for the unobtainable. The self-questioning of 'Outside Myself' and 'The Mind Of Love' perfectly captures the mental bewilderment of someone who's always used to being in control, suddenly losing that control. 'Season of Hollow Soul' is the real emotional and musical hub of the album, with its singalong chorus and crashing piano chords that would repeatedly be dubbed 'Abba-esque', rather than the bittersweet, philosophical 'Constant Craving' – simply a great pop song, squaring this circle of unrequited love.

Ingenue was released in May 1992, and reviewers could not heap enough praise on the album, or its singer. *Vox* made it their rock album of the month, and declared: 'With repeated listening the album yields one gem after another ... the fact that *Ingenue* is an album for masochists only adds to the appeal ... lang manages to sound like Peggy Lee's heiress and is on the verge of becoming the first lady of Country jazz'.[50]

Q magazine loved this new-look lang, 'open, self-assured and sexy as a cobra ... head over heels in love with love and sex' and declared her meisterwork, 'The sexiest album of the era ... normal on the surface, very strange underneath. Majestic of melody and lyric, it's the singing that crowns it, flowing straight from the aching heart'.[51]

And then, little more than a month after *Ingenue*'s release, came the publication of a certain *Advocate* interview.

★ ★ ★ ★ ★ ★

Each public figure who comes out as lesbian or gay finds their own particular method and manner of coming out. They can get caught with their pants down – or at least, their zipper down – as did George Michael when, in his own words, 'a slightly drunk, randy pop star' waved his willy at a pretty policeman in an LA washroom. They can spend a weekend in Amsterdam and then forget they've got two spliffs, a snort of cocaine and a stash of gay male porn mags in the bag that HM Customs & Excise have just decided they'd like to inspect a little closer ... They can even out themselves to stop scuzzy ex-lovers selling their story to a Sunday tabloid.

Compared to these options, the dignified, controlled, 'official' coming out of k.d. lang – in the June 16, 1992 issue of *The Advocate* – was, in many ways, something of a non-event. This unsurprising 'revelation' had, in fact, come a month or so earlier, in a blink-and-you'd-miss-it remark in a feature about her in the London *Evening Standard* supplement, *ES*, which recorded that lang 'doesn't mind to admitting to being gay'.[52] Nobody batted an eyelid.

Just a few weeks before she officially came out, some of the British press had been more than hinting at the truth. *The Mail on Sunday* ran a feature on 'The cult queen of a woman's world ... the singer who is an idol for lesbians'. They outlined the 'Elvis is alive, and she's beautiful' Madonna quote, prompted by the ambitious blonde's first sight of lang; the 'classic lesbian' hair cut, her 'rustic lifestyle', the new film she was starring in, 'a love story between two women', and, uniquely amongst the tabloids, even the *Red Hot And Blue* video.[53]

So k.d. lang's a dyke, eh? Well, no shit, Sherlock.

The element of non-surprise amongst lesbians and gay men was captured perfectly by *Capital Gay*'s headline for its story on the *Advocate* interview: 'k.d. lang Comes Out At Last'.

Even without the benefit of the in-built gaydar that some of us have, anyone with a single iota of perception should have spotted this some years before.

Even before the *Red Hot And Blue* video, the signs were all there.

There was the video for 'Trail Of Broken Hearts', filmed in Alberta, under an unfeasibly large sky, which is what lang 'grew up with every day of my life'. Wandering in the fields of gold, she sees a vision of a young woman with long blonde hair, wearing a white dress and holding a posy. She looks like a girl on her way to get married. In which case, it was pretty obvious k.d. wasn't pining after the bridegroom ... And way, way back, there was 'Bopalena' – the very first track on her very first album, and here's a big-boned gal with a crew cut, a-whooping and a-hollering, 'Bopalena, Bopalena, she's my gal' – which wasn't the usual mating cry of country girl singers at the time.

In fact, lang revealed that the only thing that had really worried her about regarding her 'official' coming-out was how it would affect her mother Audrey who, although she had known about her daughter's sexuality since she was 17, was still living in Consort, and potentially more vulnerable to any adverse reaction to her daughter's 'revelation'. She did, however, alert her record company to what the *Advocate* interview contained. Despite an initial reaction of 'oh shit', they fully supported their artist and, to this day, consider that her coming-out had no adverse effect on her subsequent career.

Choosing to come out publicly in a US gay magazine initially seemed too obvious a way to do it, but it wasn't necessarily an accurate reflection of her relationship with the gay press or the wider, grassroots lesbian and gay community. To date, she has only ever given one interview to the gay press in Britain, way back in 1992, as part of the promotion for *Salmonberries*. But then, she has always maintained she's an artist first. 'I don't consider my homosexuality a political thing. I consider it a sexual and spiritual thing. I only started going to political rallies to meet women'.[54]

Political or not, her coming-out at such a crucial point in her career actually set off a chain reaction where a steady trickle of small-to-medium status, mostly American female artists, felt confident about being open about their sexuality, from Janis Ian, via Sophie Ward, through to Anne Heche. And, of course, there

DUETTING WITH ANDY BELL AT THE 1993 BRIT AWARDS

was Melissa Etheridge, a fellow multi-Grammy winner and no stranger herself to speculation about her private life, who chose the lesbian and gay Triangle Ball, held in Washington on the evening of President Clinton's 1993 inauguration, to open up her closet – with k.d. lang standing right by her side.

★ ★ ★ ★ ★ ★

Ingenue ensured that k.d. lang again featured heavily in the Grammy Award nominations, including Record of the Year and Song of the Year. In the end, she scooped the Best Pop Vocal Performance by a Female gong for 'Constant Craving'.

Elsewhere, she was also in with a chance of more trophies. In the UK, she had received a Brit Award nomination for Best International Solo Artist but, according to lang, this alone wasn't enough to convince the organizers that she should be able to perform at the awards ceremony. 'They said the only way we'll have her is if she does a duet with Andy Bell ... I just thought, what on earth do we have in common?'[55] It was screamingly obvious what the thinking was, of course – 'hey, let's stick these two queers on together, even though their voices and music are probably totally incompatible ...' This called for a suitable retort, and lang came up with the cracking idea that her duet with the Erasure frontman should consist of the seventies gay disco anthem 'No More Tears (Enough Is Enough)', by queen heroines Donna Summer (lapsed) and Barbra Streisand.

On paper, it was a mouthwatering prospect; but when they performed it at the Brit Awards ceremony in February 1993, it showed how right her initial reaction – what do we have in common? – was. Bell looked awkward, their voices didn't really mix well, and, despite lang's best efforts, there was a distinct lack of onstage chemistry between them. However, as far as lang was concerned, it did the job of making one hell of an impact and, as things turned out, symbolically shoving two-fingers up at the Brit organizers who had been sceptical about having a mere multi-Grammy winner on the show: 'It was quirky. There's these two homos on TV singing this song and it was good enough and weird enough to make it interesting enough for people.'[56]

Causing this very British 'coo' had certainly interested 'enough people': *Ingenue* had enjoyed a modest spell in the UK album charts when it was first released but, on the back of the Brits appearance, broadcast to a primetime TV audience, the album screeched back into the charts in March 1993, from nowhere to no. 6, finally peaking at no. 3, and eventually going gold after spending a total of 34 weeks on the chart. 'Constant Craving' reached no. 15 in the pop singles chart. In the States *Ingenue* would eventually go platinum, after a similarly slow start.

But the impact made by her Brit Award performance was but nought compared to the effect an altogether more static performance was to have on her career and her celebrity status: *that* cover of *Vanity Fair*.

Photographer Herb Ritts called the images that would accompany the magazine's major feature on lang, 'a tongue-in-cheek piece of Americana with a sexy, modern-day twist. k.d. is such a great sport, she was willing to try things.'[57] Oh, come on – how many dykes *would* turn up their noses at the chance to fake being 'serviced' by a gorgeous woman who was then the world's most sought-after supermodel?

lang herself came up with the campy idea of posing while being 'shaved' by a woman – Ritts came up with the woman: Cindy Crawford. But when the cover became a double-celebrity image, there was just a hint of dissatisfaction from one quarter: 'I thought I could take the cover myself',[58] lang said later. Obviously, being just *Miss Chatelaine* 1988 – she had been the Canadian women's magazine's cover girl in January of that year – wasn't enough; she wanted to be *Miss Vanity Fair*, without any supporting cast.

In hindsight, it's obvious that, despite the *Advocate* interview, the *Vanity Fair* cover and feature was effectively k.d. lang's coming-out proper to mainstream middle America and, in Britain, the middle-class straight liberal audience. Only this time, there was to be no consideration about the possible effects on anyone back home – and, according to lang, her mother was not entirely amused by the *Vanity Fair* antics: 'She didn't say anything – she was mad at me'.[59]

Towards the end of 1993, with the hoo-ha from the *Vanity Fair* cover still rumbling away, what had been the 'Year of k.d. lang' was topped off with another pivotal performance which sealed her status as a genuine A-list star – with the added bonus of royal approval into the bargain. To mark World AIDS Day that year, George Michael decided to organise a big-name benefit concert, at which the Princess of Wales, then patron of several British AIDS charities, agreed to be present. For *The Concert Of Hope*, Michael opted for a small line-up of solo performers who had no problems holding an audience of 10,000-plus at Wembley Arena on their own. Despite his toe-curling 'Lord's Prayer' performance at the Freddie Mercury tribute, the previous major musical AIDS fundraiser, David Bowie was chosen as compere for the evening, while George Michael, Simply Red's Mick Hucknall and lang would perform small, greatest-hits sets. Though she was, in theory, 'bottom of the bill', none of the 12,000 people who shelled out £35 each for their tickets noticed on the night. The only sour note in an awesome vocal display, which included 'Crying', 'Constant Craving' and 'Just Keep Me Moving', was the godawful wraparound cream-coloured outfit which she wore for the occasion. 'Turin Shroud', 'upside-down judo kit', 'my dad's old pyjamas', 'a bag lady's chuck-outs' – these have been some of the kinder efforts made to describe the shapeless monstrosity.

Still, it had worked: once again, lang's image had got her talked about, written about, *noticed* – Princess Diana, to whom all the artists were introduced at the concert, could have told her that's what those sort of outfits were designed for.

That's what happened when you became famous – you got a reputation. And k.d. lang's reputation was getting bigger, every day, in every which way.

DYKE–U–LIKE, WELL, YOU WOULD WOULDN'T YOU?

This year's model

You must have heard the old joke: there are actually only 20 lesbians in the world. And they've all slept with each other. And if they haven't slept with each other, then they're all best buddies – right? Of course.

With the ascendance of k.d. lang to the upper echelons of fame, and her confirmation as a lesbian icon, she became the central point – a kind of 'Patient Zero', if you like – around whom every other lesbian celebrity orbited. Or, at least, that's how the mainstream media saw her.

A combination of good PR, fortuitous timing and a great album had turned her into a celebrity and an icon – which is usually the very point in a musician's career at which their music becomes secondary to their status, especially for gay icons.

It was that wise old bird Simon Napier-Bell, former manager of Wham!, The Yardbirds and T Rex, who observed, 'The progression from making a few trivial bits of music to becoming a legend is the amount of sleaze which can be hung around your neck. I don't think anyone in the rock industry has become a legend without sleaze. First you write your music and put out a few records and get some hits, then someone digs up the dirt and you become a legend'.[60]

With lang, digging up the dirt wasn't so simple: her sexuality couldn't be exposed, since she'd outed herself. She was upfront about her beliefs. She was drop-dead gorgeous, and very much her own woman, with no Svengali-like puppet-master controlling her career. There was only one possible area of sleaze that could be milked from such an all-organic, no-leather, no-smoking, fresh-faced vegetarian pop star: her relationships. The fact that she was a major talent, a multi-Grammy winner became irrelevant to most of the straight media as they struggled to come to terms with the concept that there was more than one type of lesbian in the world - and more than one lesbian celebrity. k.d. lang became the figurehead for the press-fuelled 'phenomenon' of lesbian chic.

In their rush to keep up with the competition, some just couldn't be bothered to check the finer details before they went to print. A fine example of such great British journalism was the *Guardian*'s Pass Notes column on k.d. lang. According to this, her recording career began with *Lariat* (wrong). Her 'acting debut was a five-second nude scene' in *Salmonberries* (wrong again).[61]

But most telling was the reference the column made to k.d. lang being 'romantically linked' to Martina Navratilova, probably the only other lesbian *Guardian* hacks were aware of at the time. This was a 'story' started by *Newsday* columnist Liz Smith in 1993, and picked up on by the British tabloids, as further proof of the old 'only twenty lesbians' myth. Never mind the 'just good friends' denials – this was the lesbian coupling that the press craved, constantly.

A few weeks after k.d. scooped her Grammys, they were reporting that Martina had dumped her girlfriend Cindy Nelson for 'the tough award-winning singer' ('tough' is British press-speak for 'a bit butch-looking', in case you didn't twig).[62] Then, came the 'proof' they'd been looking for: a paparazzi photo taken in Los Angeles showed Martina and k.d. on their way to play pool at the Los Angeles Athletic Club, accompanied by a 'burly minder' – who was actually shorter than both of her companions, but, still, don't let that stand in the way of a good story ...

The most hilarious gaffe was one story which had it that Martina had named her favourite dog, KD, after her new 'girlfriend'. If the hacks responsible for this had bothered to do just the teeniest bit of background research, they would have discovered that the little Chihuahua known as 'KD' – ironically named, given his diminutive size – was quite an elderly gent by the time his lower-cased namesake met Martina, given that he was her oldest dog. But, hey – don't let that stand in the way ...

A year later, Martina was playing Jana Novotna in the 1994 Wimbledon quarter-finals. In the players' guest box, alongside Martina's coach and her latest girlfriend, fashion PR Danda Jaroljmek, were two friends kindly described by Martina's biographer Adrienne Blue as 'two overweight women nobody in the media knew'. According to Blue, a Martina devotee assured her they were the couple who house-sat for Martina when she wasn't in Aspen. Once Blue recognised who one of the 'overweight women' was by her admittance badge ID, she decided that k.d. — for it was she — was actually 'more elegant and slimmer than in publicity photos ...'[63]

There was one small mercy: when Martina admitted she might like to have a baby after retiring from tennis, the press didn't suggest k.d. as a prospective 'father'.

But still, any dyke with a smidgeon of fame found themselves, as the old euphemism goes, 'romantically linked'. Guinevere Turner, star of indie dyke films, *Go Fish* and *The Watermelon Woman*, also found herself having to issue 'we're just good friends' statements in interviews, when rumours started circulating that she and k.d. had been seen on numerous occasions in New York dyke club, Meow Mix.

In the late nineties, Cuban singer Albita Roderiguez, with her slicked-back hair, androgynous appearance and carefully-coutured outfits, has been dubbed by some US magazines as, 'the Cuban k.d. lang' — even though she says she's not actually a lesbian. Her fans include — here we go again — Liza Minnelli and Madonna who got her to perform at her birthday party in August 1994, and is on record as saying 'If I died, I'd want to be reincarnated as Albita'.[64]

Roderiguez's stylist was former drug rehab clinic habituee turned 'image consultant', Ingrid Casares, who joined Madonna for *Sex*, after allegedly dumping Sandra Bernhard for La Ciccone. During the mid-nineties, Casares was the designer dyke famous for being a famous designer dyke — all fame and no claim. She was the co-owner of Miami Beach club Liquid, favoured by Versace, which became infamous when Andrew Cunanan was allegedly seen there the night before he shot dead the designer outside his Miami Beach mansion in July 1997. As well as very publicly consorting with Bernhard and Madonna, Casares was also seen in New York with ... k.d. lang. 'These are very special relationships', Casares told *Vanity Fair*, 'they just happen to be with high-profile people.'[65]

With lesbian chic at its chicest, and made-to-measure designer dykes tumbling out of closets on both sides of the Atlantic, a gal-pal was the coveted accessory of the day for trend-following women. It was a sign of the times: once, it was enough to wear a matching bag and fag. Now, toyboys were upstaged by tomboys.

Take Liza Minnelli: no doubt it was all just a big coincidence that whenever a papparazzi happened to pap her in the nineties, there was often a Sandy Bernhard or a Madonna or a kd, right alongside her. She appears to have become to dykes what her mother Judy Garland was to queens. One amusing side-effect of this was that she featured high up on the list of possible candidates for the *Ingenue* inspiration, along with the usual suspects: Madonna, Melissa Etheridge and Martina Navratilova.

Sandra Bernhard, who knows a thing or two about such matters, observed: 'All the straight girls want to fuck k.d. lang because they have this big fantasy that she's a big dude.'[66] Interestingly, La Bernhard was one of the few names to be 'romantically linked' to lang – but then she was upfront about her imperviousness to kd's undoubted charms: 'Maybe lesbians get into her, but you know, I don't consider myself a lesbian ... '[67]

Maybe not. But Sandy knew all about the dangers of being a gal-pal to a latterday icon. True, there were the supporting stints in *Roseanne* (where her character Nancy came out) and *Chicago Hope*, albums, books, sell-out US tours of her one-woman shows, documentary profiles. Yet for most of the nineties, the same-old-same-old interviews tended to focus on one thing: her relationship with Madonna. And there's no doubt who benefited more from this little episode in the long run.

Madonna became Madonna-and-child, resurrected her film career with *Evita*, got her first UK no. 1 for more than five years with 'Frozen', produced *Ray Of Light*, one of the best albums of 1998, which lead to her becoming a multi-Grammy nominee for the first time in years.

And for Sandy?

No lead film roles, no hit albums, no series of her own. Nope – as far as most of Hollywood is concerned, she will always be just 'that dyke friend of Madonna's' ...

k.d. lang had become an A-list celebrity, sought after by other female A- (and B-) listers, who had recognized that she was the very best Dyke-U-Like had to offer. And it seemed she was only too happy to oblige: at the lesbian and gay Triangle Ball in January 1993, Cassandra Peterson – better known as Elvira, Mistress of the Dark – announced to the audience, 'You know, I'm not a lesbian, but I could certainly be talked into being one tonight.'[68] Whereupon lang buried her face in Peterson's ample bosom.

It was all heady stuff for a smalltown girl who, for nearly twenty years, had been, like her first song said, hoping all her dreams would come true. At long last, they really were. And, as Sarah Pettit, editor of *Out* magazine, observed to a *Guardian* journalist, 'lang got completely overrun with it'.[69] With the benefit of hindsight, this was something she came to realize herself: ' "Oh, you're great! Wear my clothes! Come to this opening! Go out with me because I'm beautiful" ... It detracted from my focus of why I'm a singer.'[70]

★ ★ ★ ★ ★ ★ ★

Of course, there have been times when the myth that all celebrity dykes are joined at the hip seemed justified. After the disappointing debut in *Salmonberries*, lang took a small part in *Teresa's Tattoo*, a screwball comedy with straight-to-video written all over it, made by her close buddy, writer/director/producer Julie Cypher – who, of course, was to become Melissa Etheridge's long-time partner, and mother of their two children. And just to keep it in the family, the film also starred Lou Diamond Phillips, then

THAT KISS! MARCH 1997 AT A BENEFIT FOR THE LOS ANGELES
LESBIAN AND GAY CENTER

Cypher's soon-to-be ex-husband. The film's plot – such as it was – centred on swot mathematician Teresa (Adrienne Shelly), whose friends take her out to show her a good time; this means taking her to a lesbian hooker's party, whereupon she ends up being drugged, kidnapped, tattooed and turned into a redheaded, leather-clad hostage doppelgänger. lang played a good-sport cameo role, appearing as a born-again Christian who warns Teresa about the 'dangers' of a 'sinful life'.

Teresa's Tattoo didn't make much of a mark. 'The laughs are nil in this alleged comedy, with a name cast going slumming', spat Maltin's *1998 Movie & Video Guide*. *Entertainment Weekly*'s Susan Chumsky thought it had some saving graces: 'This over-the-top gangster caper might be junk ... but director Julie Cypher knows it's junk, and to milk it, she piles on John Waters-worthy cameos from the likes of ... k.d. lang.'[71]

Still, the failure of *Teresa's Tattoo* did no permanent damage to the lang-

Cypher-Etheridge friendship: why, k.d. even volunteered to help convert them - into vegetarians. When Etheridge declared her intention of going veggie, lang apparently moved in with the couple for a week, to help with the conversion. Sadly, those '100 ways with tofu' recipes didn't work, and Etheridge remained a fish-and-fowl girl. Which only goes to prove that not every woman can be turned, no matter how appetizing the chef might be ...

* * * * * * *

k.d. lang has always maintained that her greatest fear around coming out was that she would be regarded by press and audiences alike as a professional lesbian, not an artist. It's an old, old fear, voiced by many lesbian and gay entertainers − those in and out of the closet. This seems to be less of a problem for UK entertainers − with the exception of actresses, especially those who have one foot in Hollywood. When k.d. lang was hoping all her dreams would come true, they didn't include becoming a lesbian and gay rights campaigner or spokesperson, and she's kept that kind of stuff pretty much at arm's length.

But once dykes throughout the Western world had clocked her, she was never going to be able to play down her identity as a lesbian - on the contrary, when it's suited her, as with the *Vanity Fair* cover, she's played it up for all it's worth. Whether she likes it or not, k.d. lang has become an integral part of lesbian culture. How? Where? Well, just look:

The lesbian comic *Bosom Buddies* (1991) included a strip by Angela Bailey, 'Way Out West With The Well-Oiled Sisters', a UK dyke C&W band. In the Wicked Women Saloon Bar, where the Sisters are due to perform, a number of lesbian icons are waiting in the audience, including Marlene Dietrich, Radclyffe Hall and Jodie Foster. And guess who else is there, leaning over the pool table, cueing up a shot?

In autumn 1997, the Accidental Theatre Company produced a rather lame lesbian musical comedy show, *An Evening With Katie's Gang*, a story revolving around the tensions between two ex-lovers who continue to live together.

One of them bugs the hell out of the other one: she's a line-dancing enthusiast who lives her life to a musical soundtrack consisting almost entirely of ... yup, you've got it.

A popular women-only London line dancing club paid a small homage to her first album – it was called A Girly Western Experience.

In the second series of the BBC2 drama *This Life*, one storyline has hard-up, would-be (and fiercely heterosexual) barrister Anna (Daniela Nardini) networking with a top-drawer lesbian lawyer in order to get some work. When she succeeds, flatmate (and former lover) Miles (Jack Davenport) teases Anna that she won't get the work for nothing. As she storms upstairs to her room, Miles sniggers, 'Off to play some k.d. lang?'

The 'coming out' 'Puppy Episode' of *Ellen* further cemented the image of k.d. lang as the preferred – indeed, prerequisite – lesbian celebrity.

On March 1 1997, at a benefit for the Los Angeles Lesbian and Gay Centre, Ellen DeGeneres had presented her good friend with the Creative Integrity Award, and the photos of lang giving her pal a smacker of a kiss on the mouth made the front pages again. The much-hyped hour-long special episode of *Ellen*, which was preceded by the real-life coming out of DeGeneres in *Time* magazine, was greeted with justifiable cynicism by some, including US comic Lea DeLaria: 'It's a blatant grab for gay money, and for ratings – that's all it is.'

She seemed to have a point: the episode was bolstered by a feast of celebs – Oprah Winfrey, the most powerful woman in US television, playing Ellen Morgan's therapist; Laura Dern, as lipstick lesbian Susan, the object of Ellen's pash, plus Melissa Etheridge topped and tailed the episode, by singing the show's theme during the opening credits and popping up as herself at the end. k.d. lang cameoed twice, first as herself, in a supermarket dream sequence, where Ellen spies her at the '10 lesbians or less' checkout, then later as resident troubadour/waitress Janine at a lesbian coffee house. Garbed out in a long feathercut wig, looking like someone who could easily have been recording for right-on lesbian feminist label Olivia Records in the seventies, Janine's repertoire includes such rousing right-on anthems as 'Sister, Sister, Oh My Sister'. And who was sitting at the front table in the coffee house audience, watching her girlfriend's delightful spoof? Why, her real-life squeeze, Leisha Hailey, of course.

The months and months of press speculation and build-up delivered what it was supposed to: an unprecedented 36 million Americans watched the episode screened on April 30 1997, which appeared to underline Lea DeLaria's point about ratings. However, after reaching this peak, the series' ratings continued their previous trend of a downward motion and ABC summarily axed the series, two episodes short of its run. But could its death be attributed to homophobic homicide or natural causes? It may have been a bit of both, but the fact that most of the 36 million who tuned in for that one episode didn't stay with the series underscores the harsh reality: the truth was that, although it had its moments, *Ellen* didn't really have the legs to run as a long-term popular comedy. In the UK, the series was shown on Channel 4, where it was hoped it would emulate previous imported successes, like *Roseanne*. In fact, it never came close. But, caught up in the hype, the channel made a pathetic attempt to capitalize on the 'controversy' and screened the 'Puppy Episode' during an embarrassing 'Coming Out' evening, where B-list lesbian and gay celebrities queued up to fawn at Ellen's feet. Now, while it's true to say that it was a bold and brave decision for both actor and character to out themselves, with the prejudice of Hollywood and the burden of ABC's commercial demands weighing heavy on her shoulders, it's also worth pointing out that Channel 4 had never bothered to pay such tribute to any UK lesbian or gay performer who took a similar step. And quite why so much money and time was spent on lauding a series which had previously made little impression on lesbian and gay audiences is evidence indeed of spurious logic – not dissimilar to that which prompted the whole hyped-up shebang in the first place. lang herself said her primary reason for being on the show was 'to support my friend' but regarded Ellen DeGeneres' openness as crucial to the greater good: 'Her coming out is not the biggest thing, but it's not the smallest thing either. People like me and Ellen and Melissa are just a few of the players. We still have a long way to go'.[72]

★ ★ ★ ★ ★ ★ ★

For the woman who spelled out her entire name in lower case – who, by her own admission, was '170 pounds in the 7th grade'.[73] – size had always mattered. 'My biggest insecurity is my body, being big. I have a big complex',[74] she told reporters. 'Wallflower Waltz' on *Absolute Torch and Twang* was written as a celebration of 'physical bigness and internal bigness'.[75] 'Big Boned Gal' was selected in a top 20 of Fat Songs by an online fat-acceptance group.

Of all the ironies in her life, the sweetest must have been that the big-boned gal from southern Alberta, who used to wear a skirt onstage that had been run up by her Mum from a pair of her sister's curtains, suddenly found she had become 'this year's model'.

By the time she was stealing the show at the *Concert Of Hope* AIDS benefit for Crusaid and the National Aids Trust at London's Wembley Arena in December 1993, her personal assistants felt it necessary to brief journalists prior to the gig, via phone calls 'to let you know that ... k.d. will be wearing Dolce e Gabbana. Would you like me to spell that for you?'[76]

In a 1994 assignment for *Interview* magazine, Donatella Versace styled a clutch of singers in clothes by brother Gianni, who 'whether they're loud or soft, harmonious or clashing, always make us want to sing their praises'.[77] The first picture in the spread by photographer Sante D'Orazio featured a white silk suit and silk lace-shirted k.d. aloft a pedestal-like half-column. Later pictures showed her off her pedestal and, giving the 'wet T-shirt' cliché a new spin, soaked from head to foot in her Versace togs. That same year, the posters for Gap's new advertising campaign, photographed by Annie Leibovitz, were big on androgyny, featuring Oscar-nominated *Crying Game* actor Jaye Davidson and, of course, k.d. lang, resplendent in top-of-the-range cowboy denim and boots.

And she wasn't merely sought after as a model: having k.d. lang as an accessory at their launches became a must for designers. She took her place alongside Hollywood's A- and B-listers at Calvin Klein launches, including the Klein/Donna Karan spring/summer 1997 shows in New York: she was in the front row at the Miu Miu show with Leisha Hailey, who was 'dressed in Prada chiffon evening dress and diamond-print jacket topped off with one of kd's cowboy hats'.[78]

Typically, she managed to combine this unlikely development in her life with support for a cause close to her heart, by becoming a model for Canadian alternative cosmetics company, MAC (Make-up Art Cosmetics Inc.). Founded in Toronto in 1985 by former make-up artist Frank Toskan and the late Frank Angelo, owner of a Canadian hair-dressing chain. The company didn't test its products on animals and operated a user-friendly recycling policy – return six used lippie tubes and you got a new free replacement. 100% of the money made from sales of MAC's Viva Glam and Viva Glam II lipsticks has gone to AIDS charities providing day-to-day support for people living with HIV and AIDS and educational projects – to date, more than $15 million. The models chosen for these hip lippie lines were, respectively, RuPaul and k.d. lang – who henceforth became, as she said, 'the first professional lipstick lesbian'.[79] She and RuPaul were chosen because, according to Toskan, they 'are just as beautiful as any other models. I've always resented the image of a 19-year-old, beautiful, blonde, white model being shoved down people's throats. Beauty ... is about being who you are, not how other people tell you to be.'[80]

Very different. Very k.d. lang.

MAC's products were even given the kiss of approval by the royalty of gay icons, the Princess of Wales and – yes, you guessed it – Madonna.

★ ★ ★ ★ ★ ★ ★

There are also little tell-tale signs that a singer's really made it into the mainstream consciousness. For instance, they can, unwittingly, be part of 'an important socio-cultural fantasy' – according to a member of the British Sociological Association. At their 1994 annual conference, with its theme of 'Sexuality in Social Context', Louise Allen from Lancaster University told members that some lesbians wanted to do-lang because of her body's 'masculinity and American Indian characteristics'. However, it was doubtful 'how far ... k.d. lang's public gender-bending can challenge or transgress hierarchical notions of race and gender reproduced in cowboy culture.'[81] Now that's certainly a thought that would cause her sleepless nights ...

'Constant Craving', the song that's now introduced on stage as 'a medley of my greatest hit' has become the subject of a mondegreen – a misheard lyric. According to mondegreen collector Gavin Edwards, editor of four volumes of the blighters, the majority of misheard lyrics are about food – and this one is no exception. According to the website www.kissthisguy.com, one man says his mother-in-law thought the chorus hook-line was 'God send gravy'. Another woman admits to thinking it was 'God said gravy' when she first heard it through a shopping centre sound system.

Stranger still are those who claim never to have heard the song at all, but put their hands up and confess they've lifted the hook line (and sinker) from its chorus. In August 1997, lang and Mink learned they had co-written the Rolling Stones' single, 'Anybody Seen My Baby', on the album *Bridges To Babylon*. Apparently, a member of the Stones' coterie noticed the song's chorus seemed rather familiar, and realized its entire musical phrasing was very similar to the chorus of 'Constant Craving'. According to a source from the band's New York press office, 'The similarity between the two songs was pointed out to the band just as *Bridges To Babylon* was to go to the manufacturing stage. They didn't want to delay production. They wanted to make sure everything was handled properly. They contacted k.d. and offered to add her to the credits.' Mick Jagger, by way of explanation, added ingenuously, 'I really admire k.d. as a singer, but I wasn't familiar with that song.'[82]

This appeared to show signs of a pattern forming – people being familiar with the singer, but not her songs. The music was becoming incidental to the fame, and there was a real danger that Simon Napier-Bell's theory would be proved right. Perhaps there was less sleaze involved, but k.d. lang still seemed to be on her way to becoming a 'legend' for the wrong reasons.

Lifted by love

Apart from accidental 'collaborations' with the Rolling Stones, k.d. lang has made regular appearances on other artists' tracks, many of them for film soundtracks.

Her most famous duet, 'Crying' with Roy Orbison, was originally made for the film *Hiding Out* (1987). Her second most-famous, 'Enough Is Enough' with Andy Bell, was included in the soundtrack for sci-fi comedy *Coneheads* (1993). She also teamed up a couple of times with vocal group Take 6, performing 'Ridin' The Rails' for *Dick Tracy* (1990) and 'Our Day Will Come' for *Shag* (1989), and paired up with fellow Canadian Jane Siberry to perform 'Calling All Angels' for Wim Wenders' *Until The End Of The World* (1991). More recently, she sang 'Love Affair' for *Twister* (1996) and the Johnny Mercer classic 'Skylark' for Clint Eastwood's *Midnight In The Garden Of Good And Evil* (1997).

All things considered, it should have followed that her first (and, given how it all turned out, probably her last) stab at providing a movie's entire soundtrack was a triumph. It was misfortune that her feature film acting debut happened to be in Percy Adlon's worst work to date. And it was equally cruel of the fates to decree that *Ingenue*'s 'follow-up', what one critic dubbed 'The Secret k.d. lang Album', boasting an armful of lang/Mink songs that number amongst their very best, should be the soundtrack for what turned out to be Gus Van Sant's worst film to date: *Even Cowgirls Get The Blues*.

Tom Robbins' 1976 cult novel (sub-titled *The Extraordinary Novel Of An Uninhibited Dream-Girl*) told the story of Sissy Hankshaw, the part-Native American hitchhiker with unfeasibly long thumbs who, after several years as a successful model for the feminine hygiene products made by the Countess, hits the road and keeps on moving. Eventually, she returns to New York and agrees to do one more job for the Countess, a commercial filmed at his Rubber Rose Ranch health farm (named after a douche bag). When Sissy arrives, she finds the place has been taken over by Bonanza Jellybean and her band of (mostly dyke) cowgirls. Before long, Bonanza and Sissy are in the saddle together, putting her large thumbs to good use – but their happiness is (unlike those digits) sadly short, as a lot of nonsense about migrating whooping cranes and a philosophizing Chinaman bring matters to a head.

In the early eighties, actress Shelley Duvall bought the film rights, intending to star in it as Sissy herself. In 1982, Jerry Hall told the *Sunday Times* that she would be playing a supporting role in the film, alongside Duvall, stating it would be ready that autumn. But a decade went past, no film materialized and the rights reverted.

In 1992, Gus Van Sant, on the back of successes including *Drugstore Cowboy* and *My Own Private Idaho*, was in the frame to direct a screen version of Randy Shilts' *The Life and Times of Harvey Milk*. He had k.d. lang in mind to play Anne Kronenberg, Milk's campaign manager during his successful bid to become San Francisco's first openly gay elected official. During their discussions, the subject of *Cowgirls*, then in post-production, came up and Van Sant asked lang and Ben Mink to provide the movie's soundtrack. 'When I met kd, I knew she'd be right', he explained. 'She's got that tough, free quality that the film has but with a soft side that draws you in emotionally.' lang leapt at the chance: 'I'm always looking for new ways to expand my work and challenge myself; this was the perfect opportunity, not only because Gus is a friend, but I also really admire his work.'

However, already refusing to bow to the weight of heavy commercial pressure that followed the success of *Ingenue*, she later said she wanted to do it 'to alleviate the internal pressure on Ben and me'.[83] True to form, though, she never actually read Robbins' novel. She and Mink wrote to rough cuts of the film, which was shot during the last months of 1992.

On paper, the film had 'hit' written all over it: a director with his star firmly in the ascendant, a cult book and a multi-million dollars' worth of cast – Uma Thurman as Sissy, getting it on with Rain Phoenix (Bonanza Jellybean) kid sister of gay icon River Phoenix (to whom Van Sant would dedicate the film); John Hurt camping it up again as the Countess; plus supporting roles by Keanu Reeves, Sean Young, Lorraine Bracco, Angie *Police Woman* Dickinson and Roseanne as Madame Zoe, the fortune-teller who tells the young Sissy that her future will be 'full of women ... lots and lots of women ...'.

Topped off by a soundtrack composed by the year's hottest songwriting team, how could it fail?

As it turned out, surprisingly easily. During this period, Gus Van Sant appeared to be suffering some sort of personal crisis and, somewhere along the line, he lost the plot – as critics and audiences would do when they tried to make sense of it. Apart from some refreshing Rain, most of the cast – admittedly, undermined by poor direction and a script that could have been assembled by an untrained chimp – all put in performances that suggested their minds, like Van Sant's, were elsewhere. That is, a-planet-Zob kind of elsewhere ...

John Hurt appeared to have done little more than reached into the back of his wardrobe, dusted off his portrayals of Caligula and Quentin Crisp, and stitched them together to play The Countess. The gorgeous Thurman (not the first name that comes to mind if you were casting the role of a part-Native American) did the best she could, dogged by the same curious curse that has seen her appear in some of the worse movies of the nineties – take a bow *Henry And June*, *Batman And Robin* and *The Avengers* ...

Eagerly awaited, *Even Cowgirls Get The Blues* was given a lukewarm reception at the 1993 Toronto Film Festival and again at the Venice Film Festival. This 'negative audience reaction' resulted in the film spending a lengthy time in the cutting room, and its theatrical release was delayed until spring 1994. Rumours about the film included one that said it didn't matter whether you ran the film backwards or forwards – it didn't make any sense either way. The plot hadn't just been lost – it had been headed off at the pass.

In fact, it did not appear in the UK until early 1995, well over a year after its own soundtrack album was released. When it did, it bombed, big-time, on a megatonne-scale: audiences and pundits alike struggled to get a handle on it. The film was 'perfectly self-contained in its oddness and strength of mind', said the *NME's* Damon Wise. 'Cowgirls seems to exist in its own sealed, parallel universe.'[84] *Sight and Sound* summed it up best: 'muddled'.[85] Canada's main lesbian and gay paper, *Xtra*, criticized the film's 'fade-to-black sex scenes', and its watering-down of the relationship between Sissy and Bonanza.

Away from the mess that came out of Van Sant's troubled mind and ended up on film, the soundtrack album for *Even Cowgirls Get The Blues*, with six songs written especially for the film, has more than enough outstanding moments to recommend it. The opening track, 'Just Keep Me Moving', released as a single that failed to make any significant dent in the charts, captured the very essence of what lay at the heart of Sissy's endless travels, its gently-funking, disco-lite rhythm and arrangement – Mink called it their 'Sly and the Family Stone boogie tune'.[86] Its musical first cousin, 'Lifted By Love', is the closest lang and Mink have ever got to a bona fide dance track – all it lacked was a heavier beat'n'bass. (Norman Cook or Nellee Hooper, where are you?)

'Hush Sweet Lover' is the musical and lyrical bridge between the thwarted desire of *Ingenue* and the requited romance of *All You Can Eat*. In 'Perfect Dreams' and 'Curious Soul Astray' (the tracks that, respectively, open and close the movie) have 'country classic' stamped all over them, taking a musical step back over a previous bridge, as does 'Sweet Little Cherokee' with its howling intro that echoes 'Barefoot' from *Salmonberries*.

Mink and lang injected some fun into the proceedings (something the film itself dismally failed to do), camping it up with 'Cowgirl Pride', the la-la-la-lullaby-like 'Kundalini Yoga Waltz' and 'Don't Be A Lemming Polka', an old Reclines favourite, making its first recorded appearance, while 'Ride Of Bonanza Jellybean' pays its own little homage to those 'big' Western themes.

Stylistically uneven and, perhaps, over-eclectic it may be, but this would have mattered little if the album hadn't been set adrift to sink or swim on its own, while Van Sant struggled to piece himself and his ailing film together. lang has maintained that it's her favourite album: '*Cowgirls is* a really important record in my musical puzzle',[87] she said. It was 'how I would love my albums to be, that eclectic and floating style'.[88]

Critically, the album fared well, all things considered. In *Vox*, Max Bell enthused about the new offering by 'new babedom's finger lickin' alternative icon'. 'The scored stuff is breathtaking and the songs are lipsmackers ... lang has extended the bloodline of pop singers such as Brenda Lee and Julie London ... There are no limits to the places lang and her music cannot go' and also praised her 'band that can satisfy concert hall, Vegas palace and dyke bar'.[89]

Q's Sid Griffin observed, 'lang retains her high standards ... her singing remains the definition of sublime ... the soundtrack format allowing her and Mink to step outside their usual format, as well as letting them consolidate past strengths. And what strengths they are.'[90] In *Melody Maker*, Paul Mathur whooped, 'Hot diggety dawg, I think she's home ... her most appealing work to date'[91]. *NME's* Stuart Baillie hailed the album as 'wonderful ... k.d. has summarised her rowdy past, given us some more of the airy, seductive drift and signalled her ambition to cruise off into even more giddy places'.[92]

However, *Music Week* said *Cowgirls* was 'exactly the album k.d. lang should not have released if she wanted to hang on to the audience who discovered her via *Ingenue*', even while conceding that 'the very best tracks here are the equal of anything on *Ingenue*'.[93] In the UK, *Cowgirls* scraped into the top 40 for two weeks, peaking at 36, before disappearing into the sunset.

After the staggering success of *Ingenue*, its commercial failure must have been a bitter blow to lang, despite her claims to the contrary. 'I'm glad it failed', she told Q magazine. 'It jerked me back into reality ... I mean, it was hard. I was upset because we worked hard on that.'[94] And just to add insult to injury: of course, after Van Sant cleaned up his act, he restored his reputation and went on to make *To Die For*, which set Nicole Kidman on the road to credibility and a Golden Globe award. Then he topped that with the double Oscar-winning *Good Will Hunting,* before bombing out again with a pointless remake of *Psycho*, starring lesbian chic's new icon, Anne Heche.

The only gongs *Cowgirls* would ever have been in line for were Golden Turkeys.

★ ★ ★ ★ ★ ★

When lang was photographed with Martina Navratilova in LA, she was hardly the new girl in town. She had rented a house in the Hollywood Hills and been spending more time there than in Vancouver, riding her customized Harley, playing pool at the Athletic Club and hanging out with her new Hollywood buddies.

But LA wasn't exactly her natural habitat and the green, green grass of home was calling. Disillusionment appeared to have set in, big-time: 'People who live in Hollywood are there for one specific reason: to become famous or to fuck someone famous', she hissed to a reporter.[95] Sick of celebrity, LA-LA style, she gave up the rented house and headed back home, to Keltie and the animals on the now Stinker-less farm – a couple of years earlier, her beloved dog had wandered off into the wild woods and never returned, presumably a victim of a bear or coyote.

She installed a recording studio in her house, prior to starting work on the new batch of songs she and Mink had written, during and after (though not about) a love affair that ended rather badly. She said that when she was writing the songs for what became *All You Can Eat*, she'd 'wanted to write lyrics in what I call Ricki Lake-speak '... I wanted to achieve a simplicity and an in-your-face directness ..."[96] Which is spooky, because there's a joke that goes:

> *'Did you hear that k.d. lang died?*
> *They found her face down in Ricki Lake'*

lang told one reporter that she wanted her new album to be somewhat operatic, 'somewhere between Bjork and Yma Sumac'.[97] Recorded in the studios at Mink and lang's respective homes in Vancouver. She joked that the album was 'Diet *Ingenue* ... a little happier, more affirming ... very poppy'. It's title was 'about life and all of its choices ... and that does include sexual choices'.[98]

When the album was released, some music critics observed that the cycle of songs exactly reflected the cycle of a love affair, from beginning to end. But, on repeated hearings, it's not quite so apparent. The opening track, 'If I Were You', sounds very much like a little dig at those who believed that becoming a major celebrity is every bit as good as it looks. Some of the lyrics appear as though they've been plucked from the minds of her more deluded fans – if they could be her, they would have everything, they could do anything.

Lyrically, 'Maybe, You're OK', 'This' and 'Sexuality' are pure songs of persuasion and seduction:

> It could turn out to be a disaster,
> but, really, how bad could it be?
> Come on and find out,
> let's have some fun together
> believe me, it could be love.

'Get Some' speaks of a more confident sexual attitude, exhorting us to go and get some good love, while 'Acquiesce' is lang in quasi-philosophical mood, about moral questions and oppression, and suchlike. The lyrics for 'World Of Love', which turned out to be the album's most upbeat track, were, according to lang herself, based on a short story she'd written about a crow, about love from a distance. 'Infinite And Unforeseen', a paean to the wondrousness of falling in love, features the best vocals on the album, and the album's closer, 'I Want It All', is lang at her most lusciously lusty – when she says she wants all you can give her, you'd better believe it ...

The album's metaphor, an 'all you can eat'/smorgasboard attitude to life and love, was illustrated on the album's sleeve with photos shot in LA's Chinatown area, including a couple of odd ones where lang herself looks as if she's boxed up and ready to go – another packaged, consumer product.

The product's new product was greeted with some enthusiasm. *Q* magazine observed that 'gone are the retro and nostalgic sounds of twangy guitar and accordion, the country fiddles and loping rhythms her most stripped-down but most mainstream album to date'. However, there were some reservations: 'The album's one failing is that there's nothing here as instant or radio-friendly as 'Miss Chatelaine' or 'Constant Craving'. All the tracks are mid-paced at their snappiest and these are flowing, moody songs which take time to insinuate themselves. But these are her most assured works to date and *All You Can Eat* is k.d. lang's most honest, least mannered album yet'.[99] Other critics, like *The Guardian*'s Adam Sweeting, could see where she was coming from lyrically, but were also unsure about the music: 'here she seems to be putting life, love and fame into a more considered perspective ... If there's a problem here, it's that the disc obstinately refuses to get up and rock, or swing or swagger.'[100] This was indeed a moot point – apart from 'Get Some', with its lightly funky echoes of 'Just Keep Me Moving', most of the album has a slightly soporific effect. Nothing operatic about it at all, in fact, and certainly no cross between 'Bjork and Yma Sumac'.

And there were some niggling concerns: on 'You're OK' she sounds rather whiny – which may, of course, have been the intention. It also laboured under a chorus which could rank as the most inane she and Mink have ever produced – the kind that reminds you of nails being scraped down a blackboard. 'Acquiesce' also suffers from a banal, rather lazy chorus.

Michael Freedberg of *The Boston Phoenix* accurately pinpointed the album's problems: 'Unresolved melodies, metallic arrangements, too many mid-tempos, and too much reliance by lang herself on the same slow sigh, paint her ornamented intimacies into a corner of mere affectation.'[101]

But most reviewers gave it the thumbs-up; *The Guardian*'s Veronica Lee confidently predicted it would 'take over from Marvin Gaye's *Let's Get It On* as the schmoozing album'.[102]

All You Can Eat sold respectably enough, notching up over 100,000 sales in Canada and 1,000,000 in the US. However, this album and *Cowgirls* had sold less, combined, than *Ingenue*, and it was not greeted with the usual armful of industry nominations or awards. So what was going wrong?

Call it coincidence, but, by late 1995, when *All You Can Eat* was released, the straight media's fascination with lesbian chic was beginning to wane. Martina Navratilova had retired from the tennis circuit, Madonna had decided to follow the path to Lourdes, Sandra Bernhard's 'outrageousness' and truculence had become just plain tiresome to many, and straight glam girls were back in vogue.

And, in the meantime, another Canadian female singer had appeared and was monopolizing the multi-million CD sales, the awards and the airtime. Mainstream audiences, especially so-called 'post-feminist' 20-something straight women, had grown a little bored of hearing about women who loved women – they wanted to hear good old-fashioned AOR songs again, from a young woman, about the nineties problems of trying to make it work with men. Alanis Morissette's yowlings about that blow-job 'in a thee-eh-ter' put the cock back into rock'n'roll – what she did with her mouth suddenly became more fascinating than what k.d. lang did with her voice. Well, isn't it ironic?

lang later admitted that the relative failure of *All You Can Eat* had made her reflect still further on the course her life and career were taking. 'I was disappointed in myself. Not disappointed in my efforts, but disappointed in the record company's effort, maybe, and disappointed in my attitude toward the record', she said.[103]

Still, life has a strange way of compensating for disappointments in one aspect, by providing some reward in another. On 'I Want It All', the final track of *All You Can Eat*, she had sounded like a great big, slinky, sexy, predatory cat – and this pussy was about to get the cream.

All the constant craving was about to pay off.

She once said, 'The ultimate lover will be like being alone. It will be so comfortable, I won't have a problem sleeping or feel like I have to entertain them or worry about them understanding me. I think I'll know her when I see her. I hope.'

During the recording of *All You Can Eat*, she revealed on *The South Bank Show* that fame and success were 'not worth sacrificing love for anymore'. In 1996, she found she didn't have to.

Into her life came one Leisha Hailey, ten years her junior, fellow vegetarian, and singer/songwriter/guitarist with out lesbian duo, The Murmurs, who had started life as an acoustic-based outfit, but whose current style lang describes as 'kind of Veruca Salt meets the Go-Gos'.[104]

Originally from Nebraska, Hailey was a student at New York's American Academy of Dramatic Arts in 1991 when she met fellow band member Heather Grody. According to Hailey, 'We hated each other at first sight. I was trying to be Miss Stanislavski-Actress-Know-It-All and Heather was Miss-Ethel Merman-I-Wanna-See-My-Name-In-Lights.' The duo's first gig was at the Open Window Theatre Group's base, a condemned building in Brooklyn under the Williamsburg Bridge.

In their first year together, they released an independent album, *Who We Are*, and became regular favourites on New York's East Village club circuit, as well as performing in subway stations and parks, building up a reputation as a live act who were a l-l-l ... little bit different. 'We're about singing live', Heather Grody has said. 'Our whole show is the most important thing. It's very different than what is on the CD. We can give them more than what they get on the record.'[105] They were signed up by MCA in 1994 and their second album, *The Murmurs*, came out later that year, including the cult hit 'You Suck'. The duo's early history also included appearing on a collection called *Cartoon's Greatest Hits*, performing the theme from 'H R Pufnstuf', the cult seventies children's series.

Tragedy struck in 1994, when Heather Grody's stepfather murdered her mother – a trauma compounded by the fact that Grody was the one to discover her mother's body. The Murmurs' response to this was their 1997

R.O.A.R (Rock Out Against Rage) American tour, to raise funds for women's refuges. That same year, Hailey had a supporting role in the cult movie *All Over Me*, about two friends coping with life in New York, and contributed the song 'Squeezebox Day' to the soundtrack. The Murmurs also featured on the soundtrack of the cult lesbian movie, *The Incredible True Adventures Of Two Girls In Love* (1996).

Hailey met lang at a party early in 1996; within a year, they had settled together in a rented house in LA. The same year, The Murmurs released a new album, *Pristine Smut*; half of the tracks were produced by lang, while the others were overseen by Joni Mitchell's longtime producer and ex-husband, Larry Klein. Of course, the appearance of lang in the producer's seat for an album by her new love's band has meant The Murmurs being referred to by some as 'k.d. lang's girlfriend's band' – which, naturally, has ticked them off a bit. In which case, the moral of the story has to be that, if your lover happens to be one of the most famous singers in the world, then don't get her to co-produce your albums.

Naturally, any romance between an established star and another, younger musician who has yet to make the grade is bound to set tongues a-wagging with rumours about one cashing-in on the other's fame, reputation and wealth. Who would think such things? Why, someone who considers themselves to be lang's Ms Right – a fan.

★ ★ ★ ★ ★ ★

'Fan: addict, admirer, aficionado, buff, devotee, enthusiast, follower,lover, supporter
Fanatic: activist, adherent, bigot, extremist, fiend, freak, maniac,militant, zealot'

Actor David Soul, who had his obligatory 15 minutes of fame in the 1970s with *Starsky And Hutch*, and a shortlived, cash-in recording career, once observed 'There is that need inside of us to have a shrine to worship at and, where the Church has failed us, the famous have filled the gap.'[105]

Over the years, there has built up a hardcore of k.d. lang fans – the self-dubbed langsters – who must surely number amongst the very, very dedicated of worshippers. There's even a feast-day: Langmas is celebrated on November 2 guess-who's birthday. Some langsters regard her as a guru-like figure, an example to follow, crediting her with sparking off major life changes for them, including the decision to come out to friends or family.

One devotee in South Africa thinks, 'k.d. lang is a mirror image of all we wish ourselves to be. There is a kind of presence about k.d. lang ... she emits a divine kind of energy, leaving us in awe, starving for more of her, pining for oneness with her, yet euphoric and elated for allowing her into our lives'. Or, as longtime langster Heather says, 'Wouldn't we all like to be tall, strong, committed to our dream, good-looking, free-spirited, imaginative, single, flirty, egalitarian, mildly well-off, well-known, and kind to creatures and people?'.[106] However, sensible Heather is well aware that 'the image we have of her is made up of what we see printed ... '

A lot of lang-loving is also expressed in cyberspace: the *k.d. lang Net* thinks the 'Muse created this creature as a preacher of the love and freedom'. *Bel's cyber café*, which has seen over 200,000 customers dropping in, declares 'Langsters, may our love to k.d. thrive and linger till the earth stops to spin.'

The *k.d. lang Net* has, according to Heather, linked up langsters around the globe: 'The camaraderie on the list is amazing: we meet up, we've stayed in each others' homes, created an amazing yearbook, set up numerous websites, sent k.d. gifts from country to country, tried going vegetarian and tried not washing our hair with shampoo ... what I find odd is that this sense of family persists despite kd's more recently-expressed loathing of "fandom".'[107] Still, as the 'preacher of love' herself has warned: 'Role models should be your dog or your best friend – they should not be celebrities. They should be people that you really know represent your values. And you can't know that I do.'[108]

Elsewhere in cyberspace, the *k.d. lang museum* has had over 57,000 visitors through its doors. *Obvious Gossip*, the official fan club website, has a message board for langsters to communicate gossip, opinions and news on their idol. At least, that's the theory, and that's certainly what some people use it for, although a random trawl through the messages posted shows that lang has attracted her share of honkers–bonkers fanatics, thus suffering a similar fate to the likes of other female icons Madonna, Jodie Foster, Bjork, Sharon Gless... Still, at least she hasn't had to hire bodyguards or take out injunctions – yet.

There is one woman – let's call her S – who's been causing particular concern amongst langsters for some time: she's decided to cross the line that divides the adored from the adoring. She wants to be kd's best friend and appears to be prepared to devote a great deal of time and energy in realizing this dream. More level-headed fans have offered words of warning, including one who says she communicated with their idol herself online for eight months, but when she finally got to meet her, was still awe-struck and awkward. It would appear S was always wasting her time: a few years ago, lang told a *Rolling Stone* reporter, 'Women send me their 8 x 10s and their measurements but the last thing I want to do is to sleep with a fan.'[109]

Some of them have gone for a rather more direct approach than that ... During the *Live In Sydney* video, there is an incident in which personal assistant Darlene appears in the dressing room, brandishing a copy of *Hustler* magazine. Had k.d. decided, at long last, to catch up on some reading? Ah, no – she'd been handed it by a female fan. A female fan who just happened to be the centrefold in that particular issue of the magazine. 'She came alone', reports Darlene. 'Well, she'll be going home alone', replies a disgruntled lang.

A few years back, during a *Good Morning America* appearance, k.d. revealed that she has, on occasion, confided in other celebrities sought after by young women about the strain of being a lust object.
Like the time she had a chat with Bill Clinton about the best and worst aspects of performing.
'Oh yes', she told presenter Charles Gibson, 'people throwing their underwear onstage.'
And what, pray, did the President say when she told him this?
'I think it excited him, actually.'[110]

Thank God she didn't tell him they threw cigars onstage ...

Some of the gossip posted on the fan club message board isn't that obvious. A straight male fan wants to know what sort of women k.d. is attracted to. An aspiring female singer-songwriter offers to be her guitarist for nothing. One woman admits to recently watching *Salmonberries* eight times in as many days. Another wants to know kd's shoe size.

But, of course, lang's relationship with girlfriend Leisha Hailey is the subject of much discussion in cyberspace (and, doubtless, elsewhere): most fans wish them well, but dear old S, who claims she has been told by a psychic that she and k.d. are 'soulmates', has posted 'warnings' about Hailey, calling her a 'freeloader' and hinting that lang is 'buying' love. According to Heather, 'an acquaintance who's met her says she really seriously believes she will be with k.d. as her partner one day, and spends her days waiting for k.d. to split with Leisha, and plotting how to split them up. Frightening.' Yes, indeed.

Naturally, this cracked Cassandra's gloom and doom bulletins don't go down too well with the majority – she's been told to chill out and get some therapy, that she's sick. She's also been reminded that k.d. doesn't actually read the message board.

Apparently.

But if she doesn't, then just who is the flaky 'fan' who posted a message after langmas 98, thanking everyone for their birthday wishes, revealing 'me and Leisha are spending it together', and signing herself 'Your Goddess'?

Apparently, according to one of her more recent interviews, there was a time when she would indeed sneak a glance at what was going on in cyberspace, and read messages describing where she and her current girlfriend had been having dinner – the previous night! Devoted fans are one thing; but this was too much for her: 'It started to make me feel neurotic so I just turned my computer off'.[111]

In early 1993, at the height of lang lust, there were two UK fanzines, *Angel*

With An Attitude and *Highway Twelve*. A fan convention held in London drew over 400 langsters together to enjoy videos, a lookalike contest and k.d. lang karaoke. Interestingly though, according to Rosa Ainley and Sarah Cooper who attended the convention, lang's music was 'the least discussed thing about her'.[112]

* * * * * *

As well as attracting a devoted fanbase, who will stick with you, whatever, there are some sure signs that you've arrived as a celebrity: one is when Madame Tussaud's immortalize you in wax (until your star fades and they melt you down to make another figure), and the other is when people start impersonating you. And, sure enough, a number of lang-a-likes have popped up for their obligatory fifteen minutes – women for whom the lang song 'If I Were You' must have greater resonance than the rest of us.

It is a comfort to know that there are many (and may your tribe increase) who are unfamiliar with the naff UK 'talent contest' television series, *Stars In Their Eyes*, presented by the equally naff Matthew Kelly. In which case, the May 10, 1997 edition of the LWT series, may have passed you by. On that night, 22-year-old Joanne Davis from Redditch stepped up to the mike and announced, 'Tonight, Matthew, I'm going to be … k.d. lang!' Cue thunderous applause, and Joanne reappearing in a long striped jacket, akin to the one worn by lang when she sang her duet with Andy Bell at the Brit Awards, to give her rendition of 'Constant Craving'. Joanne acquitted herself very well, despite the presence of, as one critic put it, 'crap backing singers'[113], but sadly didn't make it to the series' Grand Final. Her particular heat was won by (quel irony) gay nurse Stephen Burwell, who decided to 'be' Ronan from Boyzone – a chap who really should stop singing through his nose and give his mouth a chance. Joanne, you wuz robbed.

More fortunate, though, has been American lang lookalike Nancy – sorry, make that 'Look and Sound alike' – who was one of 80 winners in a nationwide lookalike contest that netted 5,000 entries. Nancy is 'available for Meet & Greet', and has met and greeted at restaurants and hotels in Chicago

and Las Vegas – just the sort of places you'd expect to bump into k.d. lang ...
We can only hope Nancy's 'sound' is more convincing than her 'look': truth
to tell, apart from the haircut and a pair of glasses, she bares scant resemblance
to the real McCoy. Oh, go on, look her up: she's on www.look-alikes.com,
under 'Female Entertainers' – funnily enough, right next to the Patsy Cline
impersonator ...

Brighton has its own lang-a-likes, k.d. sang and the declines.

And then, of course, there's Kyle MacLachlan. Yes, *that* Kyle MacLachlan, star
of *Twin Peaks*, *The Doors* and Ruffles crisp adverts. According to one eagle-
eyed reader of *TVQuick* magazine, who submitted this unlikely pairing for the
magazine's 'Celebrity Lookalike' competition, the resemblance is remarkable.

Yes. Now you say it, it's obvious ... So – never mind the suggestion that Sara
Gilbert, who played Darlene in *Roseanne*, could play k.d. lang in any biopic.
It's obvious it would have to be MacLachlan.

But would he have to drag-up, or drag-down?

Old addictions

Drag was nothing new to k.d. lang: after all, this was the woman who'd appeared in a wedding dress at the 1988 Juno Awards; who used to perform in a horrid suit of Hank Snow's she used to wear 'in a former life'; who camped and vamped it up in the video of 'Miss Chatelaine' – and, lest we forget, there was the *Vanity Fair* cover. Even the first picture of her seen by Sire's Seymour Stein was one which, she would later say, showed her looking 'like Buddy Holly in drag'.

Then came word that her new album for 1997 was to be a classic covers collection called *Drag*. With a title like that, it could surely only mean one thing a fantabulosa, scream-the-place-down, full-throttle campfest quirky, funny and a nod and a wink of appreciation in the direction of her queercore audience, the global convention of the unconventional. She'd flirted with this sort of stuff before – the duet with Andy Bell on 'Enough is Enough', the version of 'What's New Pussycat?' included on the CD single of 'If I Were You'.

The possibilities were endless, and mouth-watering to imagine: what if she decided to do ... oh, come on, let's make a list.

How about Jacques Brel's 'Jackie?' Imagine the fun Ben Mink could have re-arranging what was a completely OTT production job to begin with. Then, what about Dusty's 'I Only Want To Be With You' – 'nuff said. And then, there was Cilla's 'Anyone Who Had A Heart' – she'd always loved Burt Bacharach songs, and imagine how she'd sing the 'What am I to do?' line ... There would just have to be a Doris Day/Calamity Jane section: 'A Woman's Touch', maybe, coupled with 'Secret Love' – if ever there was a song waiting for k.d. lang to 'shout it from the highest hill', it's that one.

DRAG, 1995, IN MORE WAYS THAN ONE!

Now, how about some of Sinatra's 'wandering rover' stuff that wouldn't need any gender change? 'It Was A Very Good Year', perhaps, or even 'Love's Been Good To Me'. Who knows, maybe there had been some girl in Denver or Portland for k.d. lang, or city girls who lived up the stairs, with perfumed hair that came undone, or the odd blue-blood of independent means ...

And how about giving a nineties spin to that cheesy seventies ballad, 'She'. Sung by Charles Aznavour: a joke; sung by lang – a spine-tingler. Her hero Roy Orbison's classic 'Oh Pretty Woman' was just crying out for her, too. There might even be room for a long-overdue tribute to her early passions, Julie Andrews and *The Sound of Music*: 'Something Good' would sound a whole lot more than that. And then, maybe as a fitting draggy finale, how about the only showstopper from *The Flower Drum Song*, one of Rogers and Hammerstein's less successful Broadway musicals, directed by Gene Kelly – the song that's God's gift to every tacky drag queen pub cabaret: 'I Enjoy Being A Girl'. Imagine the thrill of hearing k.d. lang purr that she was proud that her silhouette is curvy, that she enjoys wearing something frilly ...

Woah, hold that thought ...

What a pity it didn't quite turn out that way.

A year before the album's release, lang told a Canadian journalist 'I thinkI'm letting go of the expectations I put on myself and the record companies put on me to be a commercial artist, which I never ever thought of myself as.'[114] After the disappointment of *All You Can Eat*, she spent the next year or two 'reassessing myself and my position in the music business, what motivates me and why'.[115]

Drag turned out to be, well – just that. There was no Mink to be found and no gems, for that matter.

'I didn't really want to write a record', she admitted. 'I just felt exhausted. Writing is for me. It's very cathartic and takes a lot of emotional investment. So I wasn't in the mood.' Understandable, given that she was now, quite rightly, investing most of her emotions in someone else. What she was in the mood for, then, was 'an interpretive record'.[116]

This meant a collection of songs ostensibly about smoking, but where addiction to the weed was seen as a metaphor for addiction to love – good Lord, a concept album! 'I wanted to take lounge music and make the kitsch darker', she explained.[117] The album had begun with Peggy Lee's 'Don't Smoke In Bed': lang always wanted to record it, and from there, she started to make a list of love songs which also, in some way, used cigarettes as a metaphor for the more destructive and addictive elements of relationships. The list got longer: 'My Last Cigarette', 'My Old Addiction', 'The Air That I Breathe', 'Your Smoke Screen', 'Smoke Rings' ... and, of course, 'Love Is Like A Cigarette'.

The smoking metaphor, she said, was 'a cipher for the real theme of the record: how love is an elusive thing that all of us crave. We "smoke" it and then it's over and then we crave it again, even though it kills us. It's all about need. Because need is constant. It never goes away.'

Ah yes – constant craving is always ... hey, wouldn't that be a great song title?

Of course, this sort of 'drag' was nothing new, either: she'd done a jaunty cover of 'I'm Down To My Last Cigarette' on *Shadowland*, and 'Three Cigarettes In An Ashtray' on *Lariat* which, as a recording, hadn't done her voice justice, but, live, had always been a show-stopper.

Aware of the possibly controversy, given the increasing awareness around smoking as a major public health issue, lang said she had taken 'great pains to make a balanced record that didn't make any political statement'.[118] She had, she said, thought long and hard about doing an album of cigarette songs, deliberating 'for a long time with my friends about the consequences, about the approach.'[119] Whatever those friends said, no one found a way to say, 'bugger the political consequences – think of the musical consequences'.

But then, it's worth remembering what Victoria Starr, author of lang's 1994 biography, once observed, 'k.d. is so strong in her convictions that she doesn't give a flying shit what anyone else thinks'.[120]

For this project, she enlisted the services of Craig Street, best known for his work with Cassandra Wilson, as co-producer and set to work in Hollywood's Sunset Sound studio in the spring of 1997. To get in the mood for this dark, smoky album, she adorned the console with pictures of Billie Holiday, Robert Johnson and Roy Orbison. Most of her lead vocals were recorded in one take, live.

Just to make sure people got the irony, the cover photo shows a pin-striped, cravatted lang 'holding' an invisible cigrette. See? Geddit? It's not about smoking, really ... But even with this, there were signs that all would not be well: Australian online magazine *iZine* were amongst those who wondered what had happened to kd's naturally attractive features: it made the painfully accurate observation that 'somebody went berserk on the make-up ... The poor girl ends up looking like she's either spent three weeks under a sun lamp ... or been made up in the dark'.[121]

In Britain, the album was launched with a showcase press performance at Ronnie Scott's jazz club in Soho. And – a lovely twist – the performance was to be strictly no-smoking, so hacks had to feed their 'old addiction' before they settled down for the show. At a similar launch in New York, the audience were given chocolate, 'It's A Boy' or 'It's A Girl' cigars.

There was the usual round of promotional concerts, TV appearances and interviews, including the launch of a new US series, *Sessions At West 54th*, where she shared the bill with new Warner Bros wunderkind, Paula Cole who, with a lang-like touch of irony, had just had a huge hit with her debut single 'Where Have All The Cowboys Gone?'

In many of the interviews, lang repeated that we should 'Enjoy, don't think' when listening to *Drag* – which is odd for an album for which she went to such lengths to explain her own thinking behind the album concept and song selection. Ah yes ... the song selection ...
There are some numbers that, no matter who covers them, just don't translate well from the original hit version. Albert Hammond's 'The Air That I Breathe', a huge hit several times over for The Hollies, seems to fall into this category. Mick Hucknall (former fellow *Concert of Hope* performer) had a stab at it in 1998, and fared no better than kd, making the briefest of appearances on the UK singles chart before disappearing in a puff of smoke.

'Don't Smoke In Bed', the homage to her earlier heroine Peggy Lee, was another bold attempt at a song so strongly identified with another performer. 'Making the kitsch darker' in this case – and it's arguable that this song could be so labelled – means a string arrangement by Jimmie Haskell that appears to draw heavily on the music from *Psycho* – a kind of 'don't stab in bed' feel that is a tad over-done. In fact, several tracks are treated to this 'welcome to the Bates Motel' type of arrangement and, like Norman Bates' wig, it just ain't fittin'.

For all the grand claims to be putting a female spin on it (including guitar work from 'Wendy and Lisa' Wendy Melvoin), Steve Miller's 'The Joker' is basically just a piece of silly 70s limp cock-rock, no matter who's bending its gender, while 'Theme From The Valley Of The Dolls' is a waste of space on anyone's album. 'Love Is Like A Cigarette' was not the best choice of track to close the album with, and somebody in the studio really should have pointed out that all that mucking about with an electronic tuner might have been fun at the time, but it's just bloody irritating when you have to try and listen to the finished track.

Drag does contain a few moments of lang magic, consisting mainly of four songs in the second half of the album. On 'Your Smoke Screen', the final lines are sung by an angelic chorus of spine-tingling multi-dubbed langs, before an abrupt end that leaves you wishing the producers had opted for an arrangement that made it last a little longer. 'Till The Heart Caves In' is a full-throttle, hear-it-and-weep ballad that reminds you of just what The Voice is capable of with the brakes off. The treatment of the Les Paul/Mary Ford chestnut, 'Smoke Rings', is a nice little touch of the old irony, while the darker-than-dark jazz arrangement of Jane Siberry's 'Hain't It Funny' is probably the most successful part of the *Drag* experiment, even though its lyrical link with the smoking/love/addiction metaphor is a bit tenuous.

Despite lang's oft-repeated insistence that doing an album of 60-a-day songs was ironic, and in no way to be taken literally, some Americans certainly didn't get the joke (and who said it was Canadians who didn't have a sense of humour?).

This was posted on the Internet:

> k.d. lang, THE "SINGER" WHO CAME ACROSS THE BORDER FROM CANADA, AND WHO RELIES ON MONITORS TO READ LYRICS TO HER OWN SONGS, IS CURRENTLY PUSHING AN ALBUM OF PRO "SMOKING SONGS"! WHILE PROFESSING TO BE ANTI-SMOKING, THIS PERSON TRIES TO PERPETUATE THE MYTH THAT SMOKING IS "COOL"! LANG, A "MODEL" FOR MAC COSMETICS, IS TAKING A STRANGE POSITION IN

GLORIFYING SMOKING AND THEREFORE THE TOBACCO INDUSTRY! IN AMERICA THE TOBACCO COMPANIES ARE SEEN AS EVIL AND SELLING DEATH! DO AMERICANS NEED A FOREIGNER TAKING THE GLAMOUR OF CIGARETTES TO OUR CITIZENS? NO!

Presented by decent people for a Smoke Free Internet. (Non-Profit Anti Smoking).

Others just treated the album – and its singer – as a joke. As a response to the release of *Drag*, *The Independent*'s Martin Newell penned a set of spoof lyrics in 'tribute':

> 'her burly swimmer's shoulders
> her open prairie sound
>
> her name, like leonard cohen's,
> may crop up on a list
> of notable canadians
> remembered when half pissed
> she might be patsy presley
> or is that elvis kline?
> i wonder as i listen
> to her new cd drag
> why she has constant cravings
> yet never has a fag?[122]

The reviews for *Drag* were modestly favourable, but there were to be no 'CD of the week' plaudits this time and the number of review column inches devoted to the album itself looked puny in comparison to the coverage usually accorded a new k.d. lang album. David Quantick of *Q* said 'You can imagine exactly what this album sounds like but who cares? It's gorgeous.'[123]   Simon Williams in *NME* thought the 'collection of off-the-wall cocktail lounge cover versions' contained 'treats aplenty for wobbly-hearted scatter cushion lovers', though castigating the inclusion of the 'sodding terrible' 'The Joker'.[124]

In America, *People* magazine's Amy Linden praised *Drag* for its 'mysterious, mesmerizing pop as seductive as the addictions lang explores', while Robert Hilburn in the *LA Times* said that it 'combines mainstream pop accessibility with torch-drive cabaret intimacy in ways that seem absolutely addictive themselves'.[125]

So, it was hardly all critical brickbats, then. But they didn't do the business and nor did the album. Two singles were plucked from the album, 'The Joker', and 'The Air That I Breathe'. Neither set the charts alight on either side of the Atlantic.

What the heck had gone wrong?

The explanation for the commercial indifference which greeted *Drag* might be that pitching camp firmly in the middle of the genre road so intentionally and unapologetically seemed at odds with everything that she'd done before. Part of her appeal had always been because she was perceived as a musical personality unlike any other, way out there on the edge of left field. Even when she wandered all over recognized genres, such as country or torch-singing, it was hardly along the conventional path. Yet, if what she's said on the subject is to be believed, this is precisely what she set out to do: 'I'm not settling for the middle of the road — I prefer it', she said. 'Besides, alternative music now isn't alternative anymore. I think it's more subversive being in the middle.'[126] One British journalist at the London launch of *Drag* was appalled when lang admitted that she had set out to make 'a neutral record'.[127]

But, despite the much-vaunted 'concept' and the artistic aspirations contained therein, there is an overall impression on *Drag* of a singer who's come up with the album under a certain amount of duress, sounding rather as though she's just going through the motions, half-heartedly winding up a seven-album contract. Even as a vocal showcase, it sells her a little short and may well be fated to go down in musical history as being from the tradition, started in 1975 by John Lennon's *Rock'n'Roll* album (and further exemplified by Annie Lennox's mediocre *Medusa*) which, according to writer David Bennun, established 'the idea that a pop star has the right to waste your time with an album of uninventive cover versions'.[128]

Drag does sound rather like one big homage to her vocal idols – apart from the obvious Lee comparisons, she sounds eerily like Karen Carpenter on 'My Old Addiction', while you don't need to know that 'Till The Heart Caves In' was co-written by Roy Orbison.

But then, what's so bad about paying tribute to your idols? Fundamentally, nothing. It's just, it's just … this is *k.d. lang*, for God's sake, by common consensus, possessor of one of the finest female voices of the late 20th century, and co-writer of songs which transcended the heterosexual norm. And yet it was she who came up with an album of largely limp cover versions. She didn't set out to be an interpretive singer – after all, she launched her career at 13 with a number she'd written herself. When *Ingenue* was released, she said that wanted to sing original material, but 'to deliver it from the position of a singer, rather than as a writer'.

But by the time it came to make *Drag*, maybe she had simply run out of things to say in her own words. And maybe it was time to become 'attracted' to reading more than a dictionary. During the recording of *Drag*, she had revealed to a journalist who dropped into the studio, 'I wish that I was smarter than I am'.[129]

But, then, what the hell, it is her voice – she can do what she likes with it, and it's none of our business. Until we're expected to buy it. And, unfortunately, the poor sales of *Drag* showed that people expect a whole lot more from her now than just The Voice.

She might well have had an inkling that all would not be well with *Drag*, saleswise. At its London launch, she told an *Observer* journalist that when an album didn't do as well as you hoped, 'it's a great opportunity to re-evaluate your priorities'.[130]

She once said 'Every record I've ever made takes a long time to take off'.[131] Unfortunately, *Drag* didn't have the wings to make it.

The tone of *Drag* was in sharp contrast to the jaunty, effervescent, flirty, camp performer captured in the refreshingly unpretentious *Live in Sydney* video, released the same year, and filmed during her three-night sell-out stint at the city's State Theatre in 1996. It was hardly *In Bed With k.d.* (though there are a few seconds of her catching forty winks): no celebrity pals hanging out backstage, no queeny entourage – just faithful PA Darlene. Of course, there was some almost-obligatory footage of the lang backing musicians and singers showing that, hey, they had personalities too.

It was far more of a 'the best of k.d. lang' – not a greatest hits collection, but k.d. at her very best, doing what she loved doing best: singing and swinging and getting merry in front of rapturous fans. There were no Madonna-like backstage scenes of lovers hanging around or arguments with technicians. It merely captured a great singer, doing what she loved best: showing off in front of her fans and giving them a bonza night out – despite the over-rehearsed, rather corny inter-song routines. One critic felt that these interludes 'were so scripted that they forced k.d. further away from us'.[132]
Offstage, she made a brief return to acting again in 1997: someone made her an offer she couldn't refuse and she accepted a small role in *The Last Don*, the TV mini-series based on Mario Puzo's sprawling best-selling novel-of-the-same-name, following a mafia family's fortunes from the sixies to the eighties, with a cast that boasted Danny Aiello, Joe Mantegna, Kirstie Alley and Daryl Hannah; lang played Dita Tommey, the director of a film starring the lover of one of the 'family' members.

She was shown the proper respect.

High time for a detour

Drag didn't become the slow-burner she'd hoped for – it was more like an irritating roll-up that refuses to light, no matter how many matches you use on it, and it failed to set the charts on fire.

In the *Live In Sydney* video, she had said the shows on that tour were special because they would be 'like a retrospective' of the previous decade's work. A line was clearly being drawn underneath matters. More than a decade ago, she vowed 'I promise to keep singing only for the right reasons'. Within a few years, however, there were discernible hints that disillusionment had set in. An interviewer asked her when it was time to write a record. 'When the record company says we need a new product', came the reply.[133] She also appeared to be bored with what she called 'sexual specifics'. In a 1997 interview, she whinged 'God, do you know how many times I've answered lesbian questions in the last five years?'[134]

And so, from early 1998, for the first time in 15 years, she decided to take a year off and do nothing that year, there would be no album, no singles, no concert tours.

Four years ago, she told *Elle* magazine of her hopes for the next decade: 'I would love to get married and settle down with my lover, and just cook and walk and have dogs ... Still, I don't know that once I was there I wouldn't be saying, God, I miss the stage.' Note the emphasis there – 'stage', not 'studio'.

She admitted that taking a year off was 'scary ... but absolutely essential ... to put things in perspective'.[135] It certainly seemed to do the trick: 'Love', she told Roseanne, 'is the most successful thing one can attain.' And so she hunkered down with Leisha and their dog, Sailor, a refugee from the pound. However,

DOING WHAT SHE LOVES BEST, AT ONE OF HER LAST UK CONCERTS 1996

bucking the trend, lang was adamant that they didn't want to have babies. The pair were seen schmoozing at the 1998 Oscars, hanging out at the *Vanity Fair* party at Morton's in West Hollywood with – bet you can't guess – Anne Heche and Ellen DeGeneres (then celebrating their first anniversary) and Melissa Etheridge and Julie Cypher. In March 1999, they were guests at Elton John's post-Oscar dinner and party.

Most of lang's public appearances in 1998 were to benefit others, rather than herself. Fighting AIDS still remains a priority and her commitment to MAC (now without its founder Frank Toskan, who left the company in late 1998) hasn't wavered, even if, as she sees it, complacency about the crisis is still rampant: 'People need a dose of reality, they need to see the disease.' In the autumn, she appeared at MAC's Nashville Cares AIDS Benefit in October and attended M.A.C's Fashion Cares in Toronto, where she sang in tribute to Frank Angelo who died in the spring of 1997 in bizarre circumstances, while undergoing cosmetic surgery. She was also on hand at the Macy/American Express Passport AIDS fundraiser fashion event in LA in October, helping to support an ailing Liz Taylor on stage alongside Magic Johnson, and in November, flew to Australia to help launch MAC in Sydney and Melbourne, aided by some of the country's finest drag queens.

During the spring, there was a brief return to work, when she joined the cast of the film, *Eye of the Beholder,* directed by Stephan Elliott, creator of *Priscilla, Queen of the Desert.* The film, shot in Montreal and adapted by Elliott and Marc Behm from Behm's novel of the same name, has lang playing the supporting role of Hilary, a 'co-worker and confidante of high-tech member of an intelligence organisation' alongside Mr Ubiquity, Ewan McGregor, and Jason Priestley.[136]

In September, she was the guest on an edition of the execrable *Roseanne* talk show (screened on Channel 5 in the UK), admitting that she was a little nervous as she made her first TV appearance in over a year. Despite the toe-curling format of the show, littered with Roseanne's own particular brand of psycho-babble, k.d. lang still managed to come across as a breath of fresh air, treating Roseanne and the audience to one of her and Leisha's favourite organic dishes, heavy on the tofu before showing the torch was still burning with a slick rendition of a song she'd started to feature in her last concert sets, the Carmen McRae torchy, 'Right To Love' – a song lang had once sung for Bill Clinton. Who perhaps had taken the title a bit too literally ...

And meanwhile, the fans waited ... and waited ... and waited ...

The Warner Bros message board was a-buzz with rumours: she's taking a two-year vacation; the fan club is being wound down; she's going to concentrate on acting instead of singing. The best ones said she was going to do a guest appearance on *The Muppet Show* and *Xena: Warrior Princess.* Many fans post messages, impatient in tone, saying they're fed up with waiting for a new single or album. Others defend her, saying what right have they or anyone to expect or demand anything of her. The hottest rumour was that a member of the *Obvious Gossip* staff has unofficially confirmed that their gal is not working on a new album, and has, indeed, retired.

Then things threatened to turn nasty when David Maddocks, manager of the fan club for six years, was fired on January 15 1999 and immediately filed a lawsuit against lang in the Supreme Court of British Columbia for wrongful termination. Apparently, letting Maddocks go was just business, not personal – all part of the winding-down of *Obvious Gossip* – and, according to Maddocks, nor was the lawsuit: 'It's nothing personal with kd. She's a great, great person', he told reporters. Wisely, the suit was quickly settled out of court, with both parties sworn to secrecy over the terms of the deal.

lang's only recent appearance in concert was unbilled and unplanned – according to *E! Gossip* (and some fans who claimed to have witnessed the incident), it came during one of The Murmurs' concerts on their 1998 US tour (the gig's audience included those stalwarts of the '20 Lesbians' Club, Ellen DeGeneres and Anne Heche). For reasons which remain disputed, Leisha Haley apparently quit the stage mid-song. Enter girlfriend, k.d. lang, who stepped in and took over her lover's backing vocals.

'k.d. lang's girlfriend's band' kept busy during 1998. There was an extensive tour of America, plus a mini-tour of Canada, to promote their new album, *Blender*, released towards the end of the year, so-called because it combined the best of *Pristine Smut* with new material produced by Matthew Wilder, a one-hit wonder with the 1983 single, 'Break My Stride' and, more recently, knob-twiddler for No Doubt on their album *Tragic Kingdom*. Now it was their turn to start being cover girls: they featured on the front of the February 1999 issue of *Girlfriends* and at the 1999 GLAAD Media Awards (at which Melissa Etheridge and Julie Cypher were being specially honoured), *Blender* was up for Outstanding Music Award.

Meanwhile, 'Leisha Hailey's girlfriend' continued to take a backseat, and support her lover's attempts to shift her band's career into the next gear, while she seemed content to let her own remain in neutral.

* * * * * *

Four years ago, when *All You Can Eat* was released, k.d. lang was aware that she might become passé: 'Once you've done something, people go, "Oh, whatever, she's another lesbian, she came out, it's kinda boring." ' Unfortunately, her words were prophetic, and precisely this kind of ennui appeared to set in the minds of some of the mainstream press and those outside of the fanbase.

The tell-tale signs were there as early as January 1995: *Diva* magazine writers compiled a list of what they predicted would be in and out during the coming year: amongst those listed as passé were cowgirls and lesbian chic. Sarah Cooper, in the same issue, observed that coming out now seemed to ensure lesbian artists a (virtually) uncritical lesbian audience. 'Let's face it, coming out has to be the best career moved Melissa Etheridge ever made. How else could an average woman singer pedalling hackneyed AOR fill the Albert Hall? Even k.d. is getting more and more soft-edged with coffee-table book styling'.[137]

During her 1996 *All You Can Eat* tour, even some of the more devoted fans were beginning to flinch in the US, complaining at shelling out $50 for a ticket and in the UK, the price of the 'official' merchandise, including £6 for a 12-page booklet of photographs. One US fan's verdict was that 'the price was too high, the obvious money-grabbing commercialization disappointing and the music not very innovative'.[138]

More than five years after she went from being denounced in her home province as a degenerate on the grounds of her dietary, rather than sexual, habits, there's been some kissing and making up between Canada and its Alberta Rose. The 'Great Canadian Music Poll' saw *Ingenue* voted as 13 in the top 100 Canadian albums of all time. In 1996, more than 10 years after stealing the show at the 1985 Edmonton Folk Festival, and starting her musical journey, she returned to play on the closing day, with all hostilities ceased. Then, on April 16 1997, Governor-General Romeo Leblanc invested her with the Order of Canada, the country's highest civilian honour. So now it's 'k.d. lang OC'. Or should that be 'k.d. lang oc'?

In the summer of 1998, Canadian dyke magazine *Siren* listed their choice of 'Ten of Canada's Most Influential Lesbians': 'Think what you like of k.d. lang, but she was the first one to do it to come out as a lesbian ... when no other mainstream musician or actor had taken the leap'.[139] 'Canada's like a home town,' lang mused. 'They're your biggest fans and your worst critics. I still can't seem to shake the controversial side of being k.d. lang. I guess that's maybe to my benefit.'[140]

The March '98 edition of UK magazine *Vox* led with a feature on 'Pop Divas', including a poll on 'the 20 most wanted women of 1998'. Without an obvious hit album or single for several years she may have been, but lining up at no. 5 was everyone's favourite out dyke singer. And, at the end of 1998, over 400 readers of *Diva* magazine responded to a survey about love, sex and the whole damn thing. In the Fantasies section, the favourite lust object – by a mile – was Kathy Dawn. On a mountain top, on a beach, on an island, in a log cabin, in a hotel room whatever the venue, there's a woman out there somewhere, gagging to take her there.

And, despite her reluctance to become a 'professional lesbian', the lesbian and gay community didn't seem to resent this too much. In March 1998, she was presented with the Michael Callen Medal of Achievement at the Gay/Lesbian American Music Awards. The event at New York's Manhattan Centre included a performance by The Murmurs. Later that same month, again in New York, she was the recipient of the GLAAD Vito Russo Entertainer Award, presented to 'an openly lesbian or gay individual who has achieved excellence in a specific area of media and has furthered the visibility and understanding of the lesbian, gay, bisexual and transgender community through his/her work'.

Fine. But, going from a triple Grammy-winner to a popular lust object – was that what nearly 15 years grafting away at her music had all been for?

In the beginning, her image had gone against her and harmed her sales and her airplay in the country market. Then the awards started coming, and the image and the music changed. She became the big star she'd always wanted to be. How ironic then, especially for the queen of irony, that things came full circle: the image was accepted – and then some – but the airplay and the sales had taken a sharp nosedive.

Longtime lang fan Heather Playle, a communications product manager and marketer by trade, believes the problem lies with all concerned with the artist formerly known as Kathy – management, record company and, to an extent, the artist herself. Playle's professional view is that 'Unlike most consumer products, k.d. has more unique selling points (USPs) than any other product, service or artist I've ever come across. Every year she presents you with a new product differentiation, a new theme, and a whole new market to go after. All the while, her base (gay) audience remains faithful, so you always have a reliable market to build from - *if* you look after them by putting programmes together that make them feel special.' Well, that all looks sound on paper. So, what could the problem be? According to Playle, 'Warner's don't play to her strengths, they don't capitalise on her themes, they don't think originally, they don't research their markets, they don't tap into her creative energy. As a result, many of the people who buy her one year don't continue to do so the next.' The dwindling sales of each album since *Ingenue* certainly give weight to this theory. But the blame can't be laid entirely at Warner Bros' door. 'k.d. could still have the most enjoyable, profitable part of her career before her, but if that's what she wants, I truly doubt she'll achieve it unless she hires people who share her aspirations ... '[141] Playle admits that 'I've mostly stopped buying k.d. stuff and lost a lot of the respect I once had for her. I know I'm not the only one by a long shot.'[142]

Whatever lang's own attitude towards her career, the whole vexing issue of how major record companies go about marketing – or not, in some cases – their quirkier artists comes into play more significantly when it's queer-identified women they're dealing with. Several such female singers, with talent and potential in abundance, have seemed well on their way to the top, when they crunched into a glass ceiling.

Scottish singer Horse boasts a fine voice and can write what critics would embrace as 'pop tunes'. Her gender-unspecific name (she's even had it on all her bank cards) is topped off with an image some way butcher than lang's — she admits she's often been mistaken for a man by audiences and DJs alike. On the back of her critically-acclaimed debut album *The Same Sky*, released in 1990, she and her band did major tours with the likes of Aztec Camera and Tina Turner. But the voice and the tunes haven't brought about a feeding frenzy for Horse's music or image. Was she simply not big enough for the big time — or vice versa?

Then there is Black singer Me'Shell Ndegeocello, who was signed by Madonna's Maverick label in 1992 — coincidentally (or maybe not?) the very same year that saw lesbian chic, kd's coming out and *Ingenue*. With no less than four Grammy nominations, the big time beckoned. Then it stopped doing that, and stuck two fingers up at her instead.

Me'Shell was replaced as Maverick's great white hope (no pun intended) by ... Alanis Morissette. Aw — those bloody Canadians, eh?

In the summer of 1996, long after she'd parted company with Maverick, Me'Shell was promoting her album *Peace Beyond Passion* in England. She discovered that nearly every interviewer still only had two lines of questioning: one was, 'tell us about Madonna' (Sandra Bernhard would know that one) and the other was 'are you a lesbian?'[143]

The truth is that, by the end of the nineties, mainstream media and public fascination with famous lesbians had somewhat faded, and those who had put their careers at risk found that, outside of the lesbian and gay communities, they were receiving a less than warm embrace. Hollywood couldn't cope with Sandra Bernhard (who, of course, absolutely was 'not a lesbian'): after her stint as the resident dyke in *Roseanne*, she starred in one ill-fated independent movie, had a baby, and went back on tour in 1998 with a successful new one-woman show, *I'm Still Here ... Damn It!* – a title which bore more than a hint of anger about what had happened to her career in the late nineties. And, call it coincidence if you must, she has taken steps to distance herself even further from the 'lesbian chic' tag: in the summer of 1998, she told *Out* magazine, 'I don't care to define myself as a lesbian. I hate that word. It's a nasty, dirty word. It's not a glamorous word. It's not a sexy word. It's dry. It's colourless.'[144]

Whoops – there goes the lesbian hardcore fanbase...

In November 1998, Anne Heche and Ellen DeGeneres announced in the *LA Times* that they were leaving Hollywood's 'insensitive and discriminatory' film industry because it had 'turned against them'. Which also seemed to include the industry's audiences: in the summer of 1998, Disney, the producers of *Six Days, Seven Nights*, the action-romance pairing Heche and Harrison Ford, canvassed potential movie-goers about why they were choosing not to see the film. An astonishing 68 per cent of those polled apparently said that they had been put off because Heche was playing Ford's love interest. One film journalist reported that everyone he talked to in Hollywood about Heche and DeGeneres 'had become sick of them both'.[145]

And so, despite their agents' claims to the contrary, the couple said they had put their $3.5 million house in LA up for sale, dumped their respective agents and publicists and weren't returning to Hollywood for at least a year. 'Everything that I ever feared happened to me', said DeGeneres. 'I lost my show. I've been attacked like hell.' It looked like lang's fears for her old pal had happened, too. A year before, she told an interviewer: 'It's very important for them [DeGeneres and Heche] never to show weakness about their decision, because the masses are like hounds. And if they see one moment of vulnerability, it's over.'[146]

And sometimes, appreciation from those you'd think are more likely to give it isn't always forthcoming, either. In writer Paul Russell's coffee-table book *The Gay 100* (Citadel Press, 1995) are listed 'the most influential gay men and lesbians, past and present' ... And, what do you know? Martina's in there at at

76. But Madonna (who isn't even a dyke), after a dalliance with lesbian chic, ranks at no. 99. Liberace, who in the fifties successfully sued a British newspaper for daring to suggest that he was less than 100% heterosexual, is also listed. (What the hell was his influence? Helping to revitalize the candelabra market?) But for k.d. lang, the first major female music star to publicly come out as a lesbian, a multi-Grammy winner, there was no place amongst this A-list of the 'influential'.

★ ★ ★ ★ ★ ★

But that really isn't the problem. In the late nineties, the musical ground has shifted beneath the feet of singers like k.d. lang. Slightly kooky straight girls, girl groups and laddie Britpop bands — they've all been in vogue, if not actually in *Vogue*. The Spice Girls, All Saints — yes, would you believe a girl-group could have less musical talent than the Spices — B★Witched, plus the Bjorks, Alanises and Ceryses. And, business as usual — the girly teen market is being milked for every penny. Most regular music-buyers buy bum-fluff boy bands who do bland cover versions of Bee Gees or Osmonds (the prototype bum-fluff boy band) or even, God forbid, Doctor Hook numbers.

lang herself made a little jokey nod of acknowledgment to what was happening — during the *Drag* tour of Australia in December 1997, she would change the opening line of 'The Joker' to 'some call me the spice cowboy ...'

And what does it tell you when the biggest UK selling single of all-time by a female artist turns out to be Cher's 'Believe', where most of her natural voice has been vocodered out of existence? Or, as Heather Playle puts it: 'What on earth is going on when the best voice in popular music today makes sales of about a tenth of those achieved by the comparatively talentless Spice Girls?'[147] How can it be, that a non-US/UK artist of integrity can sing like an angel, write songs of depth, perform shows of emotional heights, and still be beaten out of sight commercially by the likes of a quintet (or even a quartet) of tweenies who can only boast one half-decent voice between them.

Don't ask Neil Finn — all of the above applies to him. And he's from New

Zealand ...

When *Siren* magazine sang lang's praises, they made the point that, amidst all the hoo-ha about 'lesbian chic' and LA celebrities and fashion shoots, 'It's her voice that counts'. She wouldn't disagree with that view: 'It's a huge responsibility to have a voice', she once mused, 'something you have to pay attention to and do your very best.'[148]

At its very best, lang's voice is one of the most emotional flexible voices ever: with the slightest adjustment, she can convey heartache, lust, self-deprecation, cheekiness, empathy, cockiness, flirtiness. The great Owen Bradley, who'd seen and heard them all before, said of her: 'No matter what the influence, she always sounds like k.d. lang. As a singer, k.d. is anything she wants to be.'

Fortunately, this hasn't been entirely overlooked. Let us not forget, then:

> *'It has the ache of Karen Carpenter, the warmth of Aretha Franklin, the precision of Frank Sinatra. It has range, depth, strength, strangeness. It is truly lovely'.*[149]

> *'From the outset of her career, it was obvious she had a truly great, soulful, torch singing voice.'*[150]

> *'When she hits the climax of Roy Orbison's Crying, the noise of her voice is astonishing. Both hard-edged and rich, it fill the hall here, at last, is a modern pop star whose virtues are startlingly old-fashioned.'*[151]

> *'An octave-spanning wonder that soars and swoops and slides from such ethereal sweetness you find yourself holding your breath to a powerhouse blast that raises the rafters. It's the most amazing voice to hit pop music in at least a generation.'*[152]

> *'The purity of her voice defies description.'*[153]

In 1994, *Mojo* magazine produced a '100 Great Voices' supplement, the introduction to which was illustrated with a familiar black and white photo of kd, caressing an ancient microphone, looking as if she's blowing it a kiss. The list was in no particular order – she happened to be number 52. But the choice of track, selected by Barney Hoskyns to illustrate why she qualified, was 'I Wish I Didn't Love You So', from *Shadowland*: 'It's hard to believe katharine hadn't been singing country music for twenty years.'

Four years later, the same magazine ran a feature, '100 Greatest Singers Of All Time', chosen by a large panel of singers. lang was there again, but only just. This time, she lined up at no. 100, though still up there with her idols Peggy Lee (36), Patsy Cline (25), Joni Mitchell (19) and Roy Orbison (20). The panellists said '... the one constant of lang's career has been her octave-spanning wonder of a voice ... perfect pitch, crystal tone and show-stopping held notes that defy lung capacity'.[154] But, most tellingly, her 'sublime moment' was adjudged to be twenty seconds of vocal shift from 'Black Coffee' ... from *Shadowland*.

However, the final Q magazine of 1998 included a feature, 'The Best Diva Albums Of All Time', Amongst the worthy inclusions, on the basis that they had 'in some way stamped their mark indelibly on the map of pop', were the likes of Madonna, Aretha Franklin and Dusty Springfield; less justifiable, however, were Celine Dion, Shirley Bassey and Whitney Houston, when no space could be found for k.d. lang and *Ingenue* or even *Shadowland*.

Similarly, the same issue had another feature, 'The 100 Greatest Singles Of All Time', voted for by the mag's readers. In a chart that included George Michael's inane 'Faith', Baddiel and Skinner whining their way through 'Three Lions' and not one, but two singles by bloody Blur, and the sodding Stone Roses in the top 12, there weren't enough votes to ensure that 'Constant Craving' was even amongst the also-rans. And it's no comfort that even Aretha, Whitney and Celine couldn't nudge their way into this chart. However, lang's self-dubbed 'greatest hit' did make its way to no. 44 in *Mojo*'s Top 100 tracks of the nineties.

The harsh truth seems to be that, while plenty of people like the singer, they're not so keen on her music. When *Even Cowgirls Get The Blues*, her least commercially successful album was released, Q magazine could see lang's name emblazoned in a Rock Hall of Fame of the future: 'Long after the prestigious fashion layouts in *Elle* and the *Vanity Fair* cover have faded from memory, lang, and hopefully Mink, will be remembered as having not just enjoyed success but for having made true artistic contributions while their contemporaries played it safe.'[155]

Towards the end of the nineties, amid a frenzy of 'Music of the Millennium' polls and competitions, the signs were that lang and Mink's musical contributions would fade from the collective memory of the mainstream audience. The problem doesn't lie with the voice. The answer could lie in what a *Q* review pointed out at the time of *All You Can Eat*: 'k.d. lang doesn't write pop tunes'. And for an artist who took the bold step of jumping ship from country to pop, that could certainly be a bit of a problem.

After the breakthrough that was forged by *Ingenue* in the early nineties, k.d. lang's appeal now seems to have shifted from the mainstream back to fanbase-only again. When *Drag* was released, she said, 'People have said that I sabotage my career. Well, I do, in a way, in the sense of not following the formulaic path ... But in terms of my art, never.'[156]

This is undisputable: for most of her career, k.d. lang has done precisely what she set out to do as a singer, regardless of whether she was swimming against the prevailing musical or commercial tide. In this respect, she has been wildly successful – she wanted to explore the outer reaches of country, pop, torch and jazz and, in 15 years, she has done it all. When artists decide to musically re-invent themselves, it's always a high-risk strategy. All too often, it transpires that while their artistic credibility shoots up with the industry critics, their sales figures go into freefall and their fanbase goes into permanent recession – a prime case in point being lang's fellow Warner Bros stablemate, Elvis Costello, whose own musical journey has taken him from punk/New Wave, through country and classical music, to his 1998 foray into 'lounge music' and his collaboration with Burt Bacharach. The critics might have enjoyed it all, it netted him a 1999 Grammy and a core fanbase has remained loyal but he's hardly been a main chart player throughout the nineties.

But then, does it matter? If a singer is doing what they want, and their record companies seem content to let them do so, despite a low return on their investment, perhaps not. It really depends on what the singers in question expect from their audience. By her own frequent admissions, k.d. lang set out to be a major star, not a cult figure – in the fullness of time – she ended up becoming both. The irony is that, after 15 years of hard work, she now had the status of a major star, and the sales of a cult figure.

During the nineties, she has nimbly trod the gossamer-thin line between icon and artist in her sensible shoes. But, as the decade draws to a close, there might well be a part of her that wouldn't mind too much if she spent most of her time cooking up feasts, playing house with her girlfriend and walking the dog.

Of course, we are talking about a performer with a habit of frequently changing her mind, be it her music, her image or her place of residence. So, on balance, it's more likely to be a case of 'when', rather than 'if'. As fellow Canadian singer Holly Cole, one of the panel of judges for the *Mojo* poll, pointed out, this is one gal who 'really loves to sing'. When *Drag* was released, she admitted 'I must be addicted to creativity or applause. It keeps me going. Even though I want to quit sometimes, I end up making another record.'[157] She's even hinted that there's 'a very good possibility' she might return to country and western, now that she's proved there is life outside of Nashville.

But, as she once warned, 'Don't bank on me, I might disappoint you.'[158]

Whatever she does with the rest of her life and career, it doesn't really matter. This is one Western Star who's already done more than enough to secure her place in the musical firmament – and, despite her reluctance, a genuine lesbian heroine who, by staying true to herself and succeeding in an entertainment industry and a dominant Western culture that demands and rewards duplicity, really made a difference for so many women.

★ ★ ★ ★ ★ ★

If you work behind a bar, you get to see and hear a lot of strange things. People tell you their stories, sometimes you tell them yours. But mostly, you smile and you serve and you watch and you listen.

It's another Sunday night at The Sanctuary. *You remember the place it used be called* Simone On Top *back then. Now it's called* Cowlick. *You don't need to know why, you can use your imagination. For one night a week only, the walls and the bar area are given a dyke-makeover, with posters and photos and postcards of every conceivable contemporary lesbian icon. All the girls are there: Jodie and Madonna and, of course, k.d. lang. And there's a story they still tell, about the night she dropped in for a beer and no-one knew who she was, until – well, later, when everyone knew who she was. They swear it's true, it really is, that's the way it happened, it really did.*

And so, on another Sunday evening, a woman comes down the stairs and into the basement bar, alone. She'd ended up at Cowlick *for a drink, and that's what she headed to the bar to get. And that's where she stayed. All evening. But not all alone. Other women did come up and make polite conversation with her; they didn't know who the hell she was, they'd never seen her face in there before. But some of them were new there, too, and had got chatting to everyone else.*

But, no, it wasn't her.

It was a young woman who said she thought she might be gay, wasn't sure, hadn't really 'done' anything about it, but was testing the waters by trying out, you know, 'women's places'.

And, like they do in 'women's places', the conversation turned to k.d. lang. 'Oh yes', said the dyke-ingenue, 'I've been meaning to buy one of her albums. I mean, I don't know anything about her music, but I thought I should probably get one.'

As far as anyone knows, k.d. lang hasn't dropped in for a beer again.

K.D. PERFORMING ON CANADA DAY AT THE EXPO 1986 WORLD FAIR IN
VANCOUVER

Notes

1. *Sunday Times Magazine*, May 1992
2. *Vox*, June 1994: p.61
3. *The Independent*, December 3 1993: p.23
4. *Musicplex*, 1995
5. *Live!* June 1997
6. *Musicplex*, 1995
7. *Vox*, April 1993: p.30
8. *Mojo*, December 1993: p.70
9. ibid.
10. ibid
11. *Q*, April 1993: p.74
12. *The Guardian*, March 12 1993
13. *Detroit News*, February 3 1996
14. James Walton, *The Daily Telegraph*, September 27 1998: p.24
15. *The Sunday Times*, 1992
16. *In Her Own Words*, Omnibus Press 1995: p.16
17. *Rolling Stone*, August 5 1993: p.54-57
18. *The Guardian*, October 30 1998: p.20
19. *Q*, October 1995: p.66
20. *Wired*, Channel 4, 1987
21. ibid.
22. *E Online*, 1997
23. *Live!* June 1997
24. ibid
25. *Roseanne*, January 21 1999
26. *Billboard*, September 26 1987: p.36
27. *Rolling Stone*, August 5 1993: p.54
28. *Ms London*, July 9 1990: p.16
29. *Q*, May 1992: p.27
30. *The Guardian*, October 4 1995
31. *Billboard*, September 26 1987: p.36
32. *Billboard*, May 10 1990: p.14
33. *Billboard*, June 10 1990: p.85

34. ibid.
35. *The Edmonton Sun,* August 4 1996
36. *Vox,* May 1992: p.46
37. *The Guardian,* May 11 1992
38. *Vox,* May 1992: p.46
39. *The Guardian,* May 30 1990
40. *Mail on Sunday,* May 10 1992: p.31
41. *MM,* October 13 1990: p.42
42. *MM,* October 20 1990: p.43
43. *MM,* November 1990: p.83
44. *Sight & Sound,* Vol I, Issue 12, 1991–92: p.59
45. *Gay Times/Capital Gay,* March/April 1992
46. *San Francisco Chronicle,* January 1995
47. *Empire,* April 1992: p.30
48. *The Sunday Times,* March 8 1992: p.15
49. *The Independent on Sunday,* February 14 1993: p.7
50. *Vox,* April 1992: p.54
51. *Q,* April 1992: p.79
52. *ES,* April 1992: p.76
53. *The Mail on Sunday,* May 10 1992: p.31
54. *Queer Notions,* Running Press 1996: p.69
55. *Mojo,* December 1993: p.67
56. ibid
57. *Vanity Fair,* August 1993: p.4
58. *Mojo,* December 1993: p.69
59. *South Bank Show,* October 1995
60. *Lennon/Goldman: The Making of a Best Seller,* Binia Tymieniecka, 1988
61. *The Guardian,* March 12 1994
62. *Daily Mirror,* March 11 1993: p.7
63. *Martina Unauthorized,* p.194 Adrienne Blue, Gollancz 1994
64. *Diva,* December 1995: p.42
65. *Vanity Fair,* March 1995: p.45
66. *QW,* July 5 1992: pp.44–48
67. ibid.
68. *Our Little Secret,* Joyce Luck, ECW Press, 1997: p.136
69. *The Guardian,* October 4 1995
70. *Boston Phoenix.com,* July 1997
71. *EW,* October 3 1995
72. *Wisconsin Light,* March 7 1997
73. *IHOW,* p.12
74. *IHOW,* p.87
75. *IHOW,* p.56

76. *The Independent* December 3 1993: p.23
77. *Interview,* March 1994
78. *The Independent,* February 2 1997
79. *Roseanne,* January 21 1999
80. *The Guardian,* May 15 1996
81. *The Independent,* March 29 1994: p.5
82. *Ottawa Sun,* August 29 1997
83. *Live!* June 1997
84. *NME,* January 14 1995: p.23
85. *Vanity Fair,* August 1993: p.96
87. *Detroit News,* February 3 1996:
89. *Q,* December 1993: p.77
90. *Q,* December 1993: p.112
91. *MM,* November 6 1993: p.31
92. *NME,* November 20 1993: p.33
93. *MW,* November 6 1993: p.15
94. *Q,* October 1995: p.66
95. *NME,* October 7 1995: p.16–17
96. *MusicWorld,* winter 96: webpage
97. *Q,* October 1995: p.65
98. *Detroit Times,* February 2 1996
99. *Q,* November 1995: p127
100. *The Guardian,* October 6 1996
101. *Boston Phoenix,* November 23 1995
102. *The Guardian,* October 4 1995
103. *Live!* June 1996
104. *The Observer,* June 8 1997: p.9
105. *Idol Pursuits,* BBC1 November 8 1998
106. e-mail to author
107. swoon.com November 1995
108. e-mail to author
109. *Rolling Stone,* August 5 1993: p.54
110. *Good Morning America,* April 30 1998
111. *Associated Press,* July 1997
112. *Shebang,* April 1993: p.19
113. *Gay Times,* June 97: p.90
114. *Edmonton Sun,* August 4 1996
115. *Live!* June 1996
116. *Kentucky Post,* October 23 1997
117. *Live!* June 1997
118. *Philadelphia Enquirer,* July 8 1997
119. *Toronto Sun,* June 17 1997

120. *Diva,* Oct 1994: p.31
121. thei.aust.com/music3/pow61/html/
122. *The Independent,* June 13 1997
123. *Q,* August 97: p.115
124. *NME,* June 28 1997
125. *Warner Bros,* press release July 2 1997
126. *Live!* June 1997
127. *The Observer,* June 8 1997
128. *The Guardian,* October 30 1998: p.17
129. *Live!* June 1997
130. *The Observer,* June 8 1997: p.9
131. *Toronto Sun,* March 6 1996
132. *Sydney Morning Herald,* December 15 1997
133. *Musicplex,* 1995
134. *E Online,* 1997
135. *Roseanne,* January 21 1999
136. *Hollywood Reporter,* February 1998
137. *Diva,* December/January 1994: p.24
138. *Offbeat Magazine,* March/April 1996
139. *Siren,* June/July 1998
140. *Ottawa Sun,* April 17 1997
141. e-mail to author, August 7 1998
142. e-mail to author, March 27 1998
143. *Diva,* August 1996: p.31
144. *The Independent,* June 18 1998
145. ibid.
146. *The Philadelphia Enquirer,* July 8 1997
147. e-mail to author, August 7 1998
148. *Associated Press,* July 199
149. *The Observer,* June 81997
150. *Ms London,* July 9 1990
151. *The Independent,* December 12 1993
152. *Vanity Fair,* August 1993
153. *The Guardian,* December 12 1993
154. *Mojo,* October 1998: p.48
155. *Q,* December 1993: p.112
156. *The Philadelphia Inquirer,* July 8 1997

Albums by k.d. lang (uk release dates)

A Truly Western Experience	(no UK release, 1984 US/Canada)
Angel With A Lariat	January 1987
Shadowland	May 1988
Absolute Torch & Twang	May 1989
Ingenue	May 1992
Even Cowgirls Get The Blues	November 1993
All You Can Eat	October 1995
Drag	August 1995

k.d. lang websites

Obvious gossip:
www.kdlang.com/news

www.wbr.com/kdlang/

k.d. lang net:
www.kt.rim.or.jp/~majo/

Bel's cyber café for k.d. and her fans:
www.geocites.com/Hollywood/Hills/6880/

k.d. lang museum:
www.geocities.com/WestHollywood/Height/2615/

www.hersalon.com/shrine/music/kdlang

Picture credits

Pg. 12:   Courtesy of PETA
Pg. 24:   Courtesy of WEA Records
Pg. 38:   Courtesy of the Red Hot Organization
Pg. 48:   © Redferns/Mick Hutson
Pg. 52:   © Redferns/Ebet Roberts
Pg. 58:   © London Features International
Pg. 82:   Courtesy of WEA Records
Pg. 92:   © Ian Robinson
Pg.106:   © Karen Phillips

Where possible, every effort has been made to trace the correct owners of copyright for the pictures included in this book. In the event of accidental infringement the publishers offer their apologies.